A SKETCH OF MEDIAEVAL PHILOSOPHY

A SKETCH OF
MEDIAEVAL PHILOSOPHY

By
D. J. B. HAWKINS

GREENWOOD PRESS, PUBLISHERS
WESTPORT, CONNECTICUT

This book was catalogued by the Library of Congress as follows:

Hawkins, Denis John Bernard, 1906–
   A sketch of mediaeval philosophy, by D. J. B. Hawkins.
New York, Greenwood Press, 1968 [°1947]

    174 p. 22 cm.

    Bibliography: p. 163–168.

1. Philosophy, Medieval.   I. Title.

54,997

B721.H36 1968	189′.4	68–19274
Library of Congress	[3]	

FOREWORD

PHILOSOPHY is more important than its history, but the readiest way to understand it is through its history. This conviction has governed the writing of this small book, which, as its title implies, is neither a complete history nor the result of special research. It represents the substance of a course of ten lectures, given on two occasions to the Newman Association, which were intended to give the hearers, through a selection of the historical facts, a notion of what mediaeval philosophy was about. For this purpose it is hoped that the book may have a certain modest usefulness in a field of study which is not yet sufficiently cultivated in English-speaking countries.

CONTENTS

CHAPTER I

THE SOURCES AND AIMS OF MEDIAEVAL PHILOSOPHY

§ 1

S T. AUGUSTINE was the first great Christian philosopher and, with the exception of Boethius, he was also the last for a number of centuries. The reason for this is sadly evident. The conditions of political disruption and constant strife which accompanied and followed the breaking up of the Western Roman Empire made a peaceful scholar's life too difficult to lead. A philosopher has a certain power of abstraction from his environment, but it is not unlimited. Hence it was not until the Carolingian age brought comparative peace that scholarship was able to revive.

In the intervening period the best Christian effort was typified not by great thinkers but by men like St. Benedict and St. Gregory the Great. Benedict dedicated his massive simplicity to the organization of cities of refuge from the surrounding turmoil, within which the Christian life could be fully lived. Gregory, two generations later, employed a mind steeped in the old Roman tradition and formed in the school of Benedict for the maintenance, as far as was possible in the conditions of the times, of a Christianized Roman order. He had little hope in the mundane sense of the word. Preaching on the martyrs, he contrasts the secure and prosperous world which they gave up with the desolate and tormented world to which his contemporaries were nevertheless attached. The world is growing old, and death

and mourning are everywhere. The end and the judg-
ment of all things will surely come soon, he says, for the
signs are already half fulfilled. Yet in reality Gregory
built strongly and well for ages remoter than he expected.

If speculative thought did not die out altogether in
this distressful period, it was largely because Augustine
continued to be read by a few. Augustine produced
hardly any purely philosophical works, but Neoplatonism permeated his whole outlook. Although his
philosophy is intermingled with his theology, all the
elements of a philosophical system are there. The
mediaeval thinkers were to go farther than he did and
to develop philosophical systems which, while fully
co-ordinated with Christian theology, were constructions
of pure reason logically independent of theology. The
diehards of the middle ages saw no reason to go farther
than Augustine. If you must indulge in this dangerous
pursuit of metaphysical speculation, they said in effect,
you can find all that you need in the theology of Augustine. Vigorous thinkers, however, were not discouraged,
and the new philosophical effort finally established its
right to existence with Albert and Thomas Aquinas,
Bonaventure and Duns Scotus.

Nevertheless the destruction of scholarship had been
pretty complete, and mediaeval thought had to make
what is very much of a new beginning. Accordingly its
first steps were halting and slow, and, apart from the
portent of John Scotus Erigena in the ninth century,
it is not until we reach St. Anselm in the eleventh that
we find a philosopher fully worthy of the name. The
stimulus to philosophical thinking in the early middle

ages came from two sides, from logic and from theology.

We shall understand what the stimulus was which logic gave when we remember the tradition of education which was preserved or revived in mediaeval abbey and cathedral schools. It was not in the beginning the comprehensive scheme of the ancient Greek philosophical schools. It was derived rather from Roman education, in which philosophy had taken a comparatively small place. The men of the middle ages read in the curious allegory of Martianus Capella on *The Marriage of Mercury and Philology* of the seven liberal arts previously enumerated by Varro. These were divided into the trivium, comprising grammar, rhetoric and dialectic, and the quadrivium, which consisted of arithmetic, geometry, astronomy and music. It is not to be supposed that all these were taught fully and systematically in every mediaeval school; much must have depended on the type of student and the teachers available from time to time. The secular studies which preceded theology in the curriculum of the middle ages can, however, be said in general to have followed the scheme of the seven liberal arts.

Among the liberal arts philosophy finds a modest place in the sphere of dialectic or logic. In modern times the Greats course at Oxford still shows an affinity with mediaeval ideas in the combination of the classics with philosophy, that is, in mediaeval terms, of grammar with dialectic. As the thought of the middle ages developed, dialectic gradually acquired a more and more dominant position among the arts. It was from the masters of the arts faculty that the more secular-minded mediaeval thinkers came, such as Siger of Brabant.

Logic had already in the first stirrings of mediaeval thought thrown up for philosophical consideration the problem of universals. In Porphyry's *Isagoge*, or introduction to Aristotle's *Categories*, there was found an unanswered question about the ultimate nature of universal concepts. When we think by means of notions which can be predicated of a number of things, are these universals themselves realities, whether in the things of which they are predicated or apart from them, or are they merely mental products? It is notoriously difficult to think of any single philosophical question without taking all the others into account, and the mediaevals, once started on this trail, found that it had no end except in a complete logic and metaphysic.

On the other side theology gave an impulse to mediaeval philosophy. The Fathers had already employed philosophical terms in discussing the meaning of Christian dogma, and such terms had naturally occurred in the definitions of the early Councils about the Trinity and the Incarnation. Augustine had more profoundly elaborated that speculative part of theology which consists in the application of philosophical notions to the exact interpretation of the data of revelation. Mediaeval theology was to give a still larger place to applied philosophy. But, as we have said already, the great work of the mediaeval philosophers was to realize the idea of a philosophy which, while it was in harmony with Christian theology and led up to it, was nevertheless independent of it in being based entirely on human reason. The mediaevals were not content only to interpret theology in philosophical terms; they wanted to know also how much reason left to itself could prove.

On the authority of divine revelation they accepted Christianity, by which they meant the full Catholic faith, the religion of the Trinity and the Incarnation, of grace and sin and redemption, of a single visible Church and the communion of saints. But they also wanted to do full justice to the achievements of human reason, typified in the later middle ages by the system of Aristotle. They sought to delimit the spheres of faith and of reason, holding at the same time to a faith in harmony with reason and to a reason in harmony with faith. Hence we cannot understand the work of mediaeval thought until we have discussed the notion of Christian philosophy and the various solutions which can be and have been given to the problem which it presents.

§ 2

Philosophy in the full sense of the word is a highly elaborate and technical system of thought accessible, in all ages of human history which have so far elapsed, only to a minority. Christianity is a religious faith for all men, laying special emphasis on its universal appeal and enabling the fools of this world to confound the wise. What is the philosopher to do who becomes a Christian, or the Christian who becomes a philosopher? Has he to mingle his philosophy with his religion, or to keep them in watertight compartments, or can he reach the more desirable solution of disposing them in adjacent and communicating rooms?

One way out of the difficulty is to say that Christianity and philosophy are really the same after all, that Christianity is the only true philosophy. Then, if you recognize that a great deal of what has usually been supposed to belong to the Christian faith is not directly accessible to human reason, you must make up your mind to sacrifice all this and to identify genuine Christianity with the residue. This is a favourite tactic to-day, but no mediaeval thinker seems to have been tempted to hold that Christianity was really just morality with a tincture of theism. Such a solution is not to be found in the middle ages.

On the other hand, while still identifying Christianity and true philosophy, you can suppose yourself to have attained a direct insight into the whole range of Christian dogma and so to have converted it into a philosophy. It is too obvious that the majority of men hold it not in this way but by faith. Consequently this becomes an invitation to a select few to penetrate the secret of the divine mysteries and may well be named, after those who first followed this course, the gnostic tendency. The one full-blown gnostic of the middle ages was John Scotus Erigena, but traces of the tendency can be found in Abelard and were the principal cause of the opposition which he provoked. In the later middle ages traces of the gnostic tendency appear also in Nicholas of Cusa.

If you give up trying to identify Christianity with philosophy, you may go to the opposite extreme and regard them as exclusive alternatives. A man must follow either the path of reason or the path of faith, but he cannot do both. If he chooses the path of unaided reason, he is what we nowadays call a rationalist. Mediaeval rationalism is represented by the thirteenth-century Averroists, whose professed reverence for the doctrines of the Church seems to have been no more than lip-service out of fear.

But you may choose the path of faith instead of the path of reason and base your faith entirely on irrational and emotional grounds. It should be said of the Catholic Church that this extreme is not only not the prevailing attitude but is expressly condemned as contrary to the Christian faith. Faith transcends reason, but must have a rational basis. Yet a tendency to distrust the reason and to get its hazardous work over as quickly as possible in order to live entirely in the sphere of faith has from time to time recurred among accepted figures in Church history. In the middle ages it is represented by conservative theologians like St. Peter Damiani and St. Bernard.

A more adequate point of view is attained, of course, when philosophy and theology are recognized to be different and yet both to have a right to existence. Then the question of their relationship arises. They might be regarded as mutually irrelevant. This was the official position of the Averroists, but, as we have suggested, it was probably a politic mask for a rationalistic preference. It appears more genuinely in the attitude of William of Ockham and his followers.

Yet there are so many natural points of contact between philosophy and theology that complete separation cannot but appear to be an act of violence. Everything invites to a venture of co-ordination, so that philosophy may lead to religion, establishing its rational foundations and helping to interpret the contents of divine revelation. Thus philosophy becomes, in the classical metaphor, the handmaid of theology, *ancilla theologiae*. Perhaps modern conditions suggest an even more exact

metaphor, for philosophy might be called the char-
woman of theology. She has a house of her own to keep
in order, but she is able and willing to spend a few hours
a day in assisting the loftier lady Theology.

To have reached this harmonious co-ordination of
faith and reason, of theology and philosophy, was the
achievement of the thirteenth century, the age of St.
Albert the Great and St. Thomas Aquinas, St. Bonaventure and Duns Scotus. The central interest of the
history of mediaeval philosophy is to watch the gradual
progress towards this equilibrium. Hence mediaeval
philosophy retains a great importance for the Christian
philosopher, and generally for any thinker who has not
succumbed to prepossessions exclusive of theism.

In comparison with their interest in God, the men of
the middle ages were much less interested in themselves.
It would be vain to look in mediaeval philosophy for that
curious scrutiny of all the contents of human consciousness which has become a preoccupation since the
Renaissance, or for that analytic criticism of experience
which has been the dominant question in philosophy
since Descartes. It is chiefly for the philosophy of theism,
and for the general logic and metaphysic upon which
this is based, that the mediaeval philosophers claim our
attention. In this field, however, they represent the most
significant period of human speculation.

§ 3

A glance at the contents of a mediaeval library will
show to what extent mediaeval thought had to be a new
beginning. In the course of the twelfth and early

thirteenth centuries the complete Aristotle was rediscovered, but the amount of ancient philosophical literature available in the earlier middle ages is strikingly
small. Even so, in days when books were multiplied
by the slow and laborious process of copying by hand,
it is not to be supposed that all the works mentioned
were available to everyone. The would-be philosopher
before the twelfth century had very little to go upon.

Apart from a few quotations and references in other
writers Plato was known only by a Latin translation of
the *Timaeus*. During the twelfth century one or two of
his other dialogues were translated into Latin, but they
never became familiar. The Plato of the middle ages
was the Plato of the *Timaeus* or of the Neoplatonists as
transmitted chiefly by Augustine.

Until the twelfth century Aristotle was in no better
case. The *Categories* and *De Interpretatione* were
known in the translation and with the commentary of
Boethius. The translation by Boethius of the rest of the
Organon existed but was not much regarded. Aristotle's
other works were unknown, so that he entered the
middle ages simply as a logician. As we have already
mentioned, Porphyry's *Isagoge,* or introduction to Aristotle's *Categories,* was well known and provoked the
dispute about universals.

While Augustine's version of Neoplatonism had
enormous influence, the actual works of the chief Neoplatonists were forgotten. Plotinus was not studied at
any period of the middle ages. But there was another
channel of Neoplatonism in the works of that Christian
Neoplatonist who is known as the Pseudo-Dionysius.
These works were long attributed to Dionysius the

Areopagite himself and enjoyed great prestige on that account, although St. Thomas Aquinas has the merit of having thrown doubt upon their authorship.

The Latin philosophical writers were hardly better known. A few works and fragments of Cicero and Seneca, with a few lines of Lucretius, formed the stock-in-trade of the early middle ages. Two late writers, however, happened to survive and accordingly enjoyed a disproportionate influence. The commentary of Chalcidius on the *Timaeus*, largely derived from Posidonius, with many extracts from and references to other philosophers, was a main source of knowledge of the history of philosophy. The commentary of Macrobius on Scipio's dream in Cicero's *de Republica* was yet another channel of Neoplatonic thought. There was as well the allegory of Martianus Capella, conveying the tradition of the seven liberal arts.

The mediaevals possessed also the Fathers of the Church, with their occasional excursions into philosophy, and especially St. Augustine, about whom one can speak of much more than an occasional excursion. Augustine was indeed the principal authority in mediaeval philosophy until the rediscovery of Aristotle, and his influence remained great even afterwards. Finally, there was Boethius, but Boethius is so important a link between antiquity and the middle ages that he deserves separate treatment.

§ 4

Anicius Manlius Severinus Boethius was born about 475 and lived at a time when the Western Empire had come to an end but the forms of the Roman political and economic system remained. His family, the *gens Anicia*, retained their great wealth and something of their influence. His father was consul in 487, he himself in 510, and his two young sons were made consuls as a compliment to him in 522.

Effective authority in Italy was in the hands of the Gothic king Theodoric, whose *magister officiorum* Boethius became. Theodoric was an Arian and Boethius, in common with the majority of the Romans, a Catholic. But Theodoric was tolerant of his Catholic subjects as long as the Eastern emperor was a Monophysite, and Boethius gained considerable influence with him, using it often for the protection of the native Italians against their Gothic conquerors. This, however, aroused the jealousy of the Gothic leaders, and, when a Catholic emperor ascended the throne of Constantinople in the person of Justin I, it proved not too difficult to make the ageing Theodoric suspicious of his Catholic subjects and afraid that they might transfer their allegiance to an emperor of their own faith. Boethius was first imprisoned at Pavia, and finally executed in 524. He enjoys a traditional cult as a martyr in the diocese of Pavia, which was confirmed by the Congregation of Rites as recently as 1883.

Boethius left his chosen lifework unfinished. In any case it was a gigantic task that he had undertaken, for he intended to render the whole of Plato and Aristotle into Latin and to compose commentaries upon them. Comparatively little had been completed and some of this was lost in later ages, but there remained his translation of Aristotle's logical works and some of his commentaries upon them. These, as we have seen, were the principal sources of knowledge of Aristotle in the early middle ages.

Boethius wrote also some short theological treatises whose authenticity was at one time doubted. In fact, with the exception of the *De Fide Catholica,* their authenticity is amply vouched for, and the reason given for doubting it is of no weight. For it was maintained that his most famous work, the *De Consolatione Philosophiae,* showed a mind which was fundamentally pagan with only an external veneer of Christianity. Such a mind could not have produced treatises on Christian dogma. It would, of course, have been strange if the *De Consolatione* had been written in the last moments of the life of Boethius, and its author had sought all his consolation in the face of death from philosophy and none from his religious faith. In reality, however, it is obviously a carefully pondered work composed during his lengthy imprisonment when he had no certainty that the issue would be death. It is a work on philosophy, but eminently the product of a Christian philosopher, containing nothing contrary to the Christian faith and leading naturally towards it. There is, consequently, no reason to doubt the authenticity of the *De Sancta Trinitate, Utrum Pater et Filius et Spiritus Sanctus de Divinitate substantialiter praedicentur,* the *Liber contra Eutychen et Nestorium,* and the other opusculum, which would be more properly reckoned among his philosophical than among his theological works, *Quomodo substantiae in eo quod sint bonae sint cum non sint substantialia bona.* In these works we find an anticipation of scholastic theological method in the application of Aristotelian logic to the analysis of Christian dogma.

There remains for consideration the celebrated *De Consolatione Philosophiae*. No book was more read in the middle ages, and none earlier translated into the vulgar tongue, the English translations beginning with that of Alfred the Great. Burnet describes it as a book "which it is hardly an exaggeration to call the source of all that is best in the literature of western Europe" and which "contains beyond a doubt the quintessence of Platonism".[1] What is more, it contains a good deal of the spirit of Aristotle and of the Stoics too.

It is written with considerable literary skill in *satyra Menippea*, in alternate passages of verse and of prose. The lady Philosophy appears to Boethius in his prison and listens to the account of his griefs. He describes his former prosperity, his conscientious use of it, and his unmerited fall. In the second book Philosophy expounds to him, in the traditional manner of ancient philosophy and especially of the Stoics, how the wise man is superior to fortune, for his happiness depends on things which fortune cannot take away.

The third book deals more analytically with the nature of good. It begins with a conventional but forcible refutation of the views which would find the good in wealth, honour, power, reputation or pleasure. The latter part of this book has greater originality, for it develops a positive theory of the good in which the stimulus comes from Plato, its results, however, being applied not to an impersonal Platonic Idea of the Good but to a personal God. True happiness, therefore, consists in communion with God. "We have found that

[1] J. Burnet: "How Platonism Came to England", in *Essays and Addresses*, pp. 268-9.

both happiness and God are the supreme good; whence it necessarily follows that the supreme Godhead is also supreme happiness."[1] Here we see Boethius as the Christian philosopher, anticipating the work of Aquinas in the opening questions of the *Prima Secundae*.

In the fourth book Boethius raises the obvious question how, if the world is governed by a benevolent providence, the wicked are allowed to prosper and the good to suffer. Philosophy sets out to show that, while the good are independent of fortune, the wicked become worse off in their prosperity by not knowing and not attaining the only real good. In reality any kind of fortune is good for the good, for they can make themselves better by means of it, and any kind of fortune is evil for the wicked, for it always gives them an opportunity of indulging their wickedness. The world is the scene in which good and evil work themselves out, but its apparently capricious fortunes are really the effect of an invincible fate which in its origin is the rational providence of God. "For providence is the divine reason itself, existing in the supreme ruler of all and disposing all things; fate is a disposition inherent in things subject to change, by which providence binds everything to its decrees."[2] Here, once again, we find Boethius adapting the old classical idea of ineluctable fate to a theistic philosophy.

All this has raised the problem of Providence and free will, and the fifth and last book embarks on a discussion of the relationship of human free will to the divine foreknowledge and providence. The solution is found

---

[1] *De Cons. Phil.* III, pr. x, 16.
[2] *De Cons. Phil.* IV, pr. vi, 7.

in the contrast of the temporal character of human existence with the timelessness of God, to whom all times are eternally and simultaneously present. This is where we find the justly celebrated definition of eternity as "the simultaneous and complete possession of endless life" (*interminabilis vitae tota simul et perfecta possessio*).[1] Even if, as some of the ancient philosophers asserted, the world had always existed, it would still be changing and temporal, and could not be called eternal but only perpetual; the eternity of God absolutely excludes change and succession. God knows future free acts because they are present to him, and his eternally perfect knowledge entails that no accident can interfere with the dispositions of his providence. Hence the last word of philosophy is that our hope and consolation is in God, who sees and governs and judges all things.

In the *De Consolatione* the mediaevals found a substantial sample of the content, and more of the spirit, of ancient speculation given a definitely theistic form. But it was still pure philosophy, not philosophy applied to theology as they generally found it in the work of Augustine. It served, then, as an example of a philosophy which was in harmony with Christian theology but did not therefore cease to be a genuine philosophy logically independent of theology. It was the model on a smaller scale of what the mediaeval thinkers tried to do, as well as the channel through which a great deal of ancient thought was transmitted to them. This is the historical importance of Boethius, but he is not merely historically important. The *De Consolatione* is still a work which it is a pleasure to read for its own sake.

[1] *De Cons. Phil.* V, pr. vi, 2.

CHAPTER II

ERIGENA AND ST. ANSELM

§ 1

A<small>FTER</small> the murder of Boethius in 524 there was nothing worthy of the name of philosophy during a period of bloodshed and turmoil which lasted for two centuries and a half. When Charlemagne, however, not without shedding a good deal of blood himself, succeeded in establishing a more or less stable government over a great part of western Europe, it is pleasant to think of the unlettered conqueror recognizing the necessity of restoring the intellectual life and even himself going to school with his court to the scholars whom he invited from England and Ireland. That there should have been scholars to invite from our own islands is itself remarkable, since their history had been scarcely less turbulent than that of the Continent. Yet scholarship was still in honour in Ireland, and the organizing ability of St. Theodore of Canterbury in the seventh century had produced in England a flourishing Anglo-Saxon Church. St. Bede the Venerable is the greatest name in the learning of all that dark period, but he was not a philosopher in the proper sense of the word, and philosophy had not yet revived. Nor can the title of philosopher be properly attributed to Alcuin of York, the chief of the scholars brought to France by Charlemagne, but the new interest in education according to the scheme of the seven liberal arts entailed the study of dialectic or logic, and the rebirth of theology stimulated its own cognate philosophical problems.

Leaving for the next chapter the controversy about universals which culminated in the age of Abelard, we shall turn our attention now to the stimulus given to philosophical activity by theology, and especially the way to God by reason as formulated in the early middle ages. Here the principal original contribution is the much debated ontological argument of St. Anselm. An earlier philosopher, however, stands apart as a unique figure among the worthy but not usually very venturesome thinkers of the Carolingian Renaissance. This is John Scotus Erigena, who in the middle of the ninth century developed a complete and symmetrical philosophical system.

Very little is known of the personality of John Scot the Irishman except what we can deduce from his works, but we meet with him at the court of Charles the Bald. In a knowledge of Greek he possessed an accomplishment unusual at his period, and he made use of it in translations of the works of the Pseudo-Dionysius and of the *Ambigua* of Maximus the Confessor. His philosophical system is expounded in the original work *De Divisione Naturae*.

This system is an elaborate construction with obvious derivation from later Neoplatonism after the manner of Proclus. One wonders how Erigena picked up his ideas, for there is no sufficient evidence that he had read Plotinus or Proclus themselves. The Neoplatonic elements in Augustine do not account for Erigena's full-blown Neoplatonic system. However, as we have seen, he had studied the Pseudo-Dionysius and Maximus, and

no doubt he had access to Macrobius. Nor was living
contact between the Latin West and the Eastern Empire
completely lacking. We read of an unnamed *Atheniensis sophista* at the court of Charlemagne, and whoever
taught Erigena Greek in the time of Charlemagne's
grandson may also have initiated him orally into the
architecture of the Neoplatonic systems.

Erigena's work states and develops a fourfold division
of nature. Nature here has no narrower signification
than reality, but reality, for Erigena, is indeed a nature
in the Aristotelian sense, a principle of becoming, for
it necessarily evolves by the familiar Neoplatonic mode
of emanation. The divisions of nature are the principal
stages in the evolution of reality. What Erigena sets out
to provide, then, is a synthetic view of the development
of being according to its inner intelligible necessity.

The first division of nature or stage of being is the
nature which creates and is not created. This is the
absolutely undifferentiated primordial unity of God.
Like the One of Plotinus, it transcends mind as well as
matter in its dazzling simplicity and is completely beyond
the common measure of thought.

From this original unity proceeds the nature which is
created and creates; this is the second division of nature.
It is the intelligible world, the world of essences, forming
a unity in the Logos. After the example of the Neoplatonists, Erigena makes Plato's ideal world into a
cosmic mind, subordinate, however, to an original simple
unity which transcends mind. As a Christian, if not a
very orthodox one, he identifies this second nature with
the second Person of the Trinity.

The realization of the divine ideas existing in the

Logos is the formation of the world of persons and things which is the world of our experience; this is the third division of nature, the nature which is created and does not create. Everything that exists, says Erigena, is a theophany, a manifestation of God. Even more, the reality of things is no other than the reality of God unfolding itself.

So far the process has been one of unfolding and, in its increasing multiplicity and incompleteness, of descent from the majestic simplicity of absolute being. But the process is consummated by an ascent back to its beginning. There is a return of all things to God, which is the fourth division of nature, the nature which neither creates nor is created. Things fulfil their destiny not by perishing but by being taken up once again into the divine unity.

Man, emerging first of all as an idea in the Logos and then realized in the actual human race, has to learn to transcend not only sense-experience but also the ordinary operations of the discursive reason. Thus he attains to the contemplation of God and is at the same time one with God; he enjoys a mystical intuition (*gnosticus intuitus*) which is a vision of all things in God. Here Erigena remembers Christian dogma once more and describes how, in order to raise fallen man from his sinful state and to enable him to rise to the contemplation of God, the Logos himself entered the world and, as Christ, redeemed us.

§ 2

That so impressive a system should have come to birth amid the first glimmerings of mediaeval civilization in the ninth century is a proof of the exceptional intellectual power of Erigena. Its faults, however, are obvious. It displays what we have called the gnostic tendency, the tendency to incorporate the Christian faith into a philosophical system and to represent its doctrines as objects of direct rational insight for the completely enlightened mind. In reality, something which claims to be a divine revelation demanding the assent of faith must be primarily concerned with truths which are not accessible to direct rational insight. Since a revelation, if it occurs, is an historical fact, its credibility must be judged by reference to the historical events through which it took its rise. Hence philosophy, even when it is concerned with the being of God, has a different source and method from theology, and to reduce Christianity to a philosophy is to alter its whole nature. Erigena is guilty of confusing theology with philosophy. Although his is not an isolated case in the middle ages, this mistake cannot be said to be one to which the mediaeval thinkers were in general prone. It can, however, be said that the distinction gradually became clearer as the thought of the middle ages developed.

Moreover, whatever the intentions of Erigena may have been, the system at which he arrived is plainly pantheistic. The fourfold division of nature indicates phases in the evolution of a single divine reality which first unfolds itself and then, in the last phase, returns into itself again. God "spreads out into all things . . . and this very spreading out is all things".[1] "The essence of all things is no other than the knowledge of all things

---

[1] *Extendit se in omnia et . . . ipsa extensio est omnia. De Div. Nat.* III, 9.

in the divine wisdom."[1] Such conclusions set Erigena apart from the main line of the eminently Christian thinking of the middle ages. While they were enough in themselves to ensure that he should not exercise any dominating influence, the very sweep and elevation of his thought was so remote from the common run of ninth-century preoccupations that it contributed to the same result. That little attention was paid to him is shown by his having for so long escaped ecclesiastical condemnation; that he continued to enjoy a discreet reputation and to be read by a few is proved by the eventual condemnation of his work after three centuries and a half by Honorius III in 1225. But he was not left entirely without spiritual descendants; there is a notable affinity, for example, in Master Eckhart and, still more, in Nicholas of Cusa.

Meanwhile it is not irrelevant to an appreciation of later mediaeval philosophy to consider what the roots of pantheism are. Pantheism, of course, has a certain foundation in spontaneous religious feeling, in a sense of the nothingness of creatures and the infinite being of God. To speak of the nothingness of creatures is admissible as an emotional utterance and is familiar in religious literature; if it be taken as a literally accurate statement, the outcome is pantheism.

Within the sphere of strict metaphysics, however, the source of pantheism may be said to be the neglect of the notion of individual existence. If thinking be carried on exclusively in terms of universal notions, within the realm of essences, reality tends to be exhibited as a single,

[1] *Nihil enim est aliud omnium essentia, nisi omnium in divina sapientia cognitio.* De Div. Nat. II, 20.

necessary, unchangeable intellectual system. We think of the descriptions of things in terms of universals and forget the things themselves. How, then, do things differ among themselves except by negation, by an unreality? Hence finitude appears in the end to be unreal, and the sum of reality is the only reality. Pantheism is, therefore, a view to which Platonists, with their emphasis on the ideal and the universal, are naturally inclined; one says Platonists rather than Plato, for Plato himself displays a much greater balance than most of those who have taken his name.

The balance is in fact restored when we remember that reality is not exhausted by description in universal terms. That a universal should be verified entails that an individual thing exists and manifests it. Existence is necessarily individual, and the finitude of the finite individual is not a mere negation but the limit of its being. A correct evaluation of individual existence is the refutation of pantheism, and the elucidation of this point is, as we shall see, a merit of St. Thomas Aquinas. At present, however, we are coming to a thinker who made a very different use of the notion of existence. This is St. Anselm.

§ 3

Erigena was a brilliant and erratic exception in the slow burgeoning of mediaeval thought. If we examine the philosophical conception of God entertained by other thinkers of the early middle ages, we find them employing with greater or less success elements derived from St. Augustine. There is no single passage of Augustine which sums up his whole thought on this subject, but it is not too difficult by combining his various utterances to reach a fairly complete view of his philosophical way to God.

A fundamental preparatory thought which often recurs is the familiar one of contingent and changing reality demanding to be based upon necessary and unchanging being. In the inquiry into the nature of necessary, unchanging being something more specifically Augustinian emerges. For Augustine finds the unmistakeable reflection of absolute being in the necessity of essences and of the truths which depend exclusively upon essences and their mutual relations. Mathematical truths, for instance, are eternally true whether they be exemplified in contingent things or not. And the more of value truth reveals, as in the experience of order and beauty, the more it bears the mark of inevitability and approximates to absoluteness. Hence Augustine conceives absolute being as an eternal mind necessarily contemplating eternal truth and embodying the perfection of good. It is some part or other of this synthesis which the earlier mediaeval writers reproduce when touching upon our natural knowledge of God. With Anselm, although his philosophy is in general derived from Augustine, we come upon an original contribution in the ontological argument.

Anselm, born at Aosta in 1033, joined the Norman abbey of Bec, from which he was summoned to be archbishop of Canterbury in 1093. While he held that office, his energies were perforce devoted to asserting the rights of the Church against the King in the question of investiture, but he was able to die in peace in 1109. He was, apart from Erigena, the first really systematic thinker of the middle ages. His celebrated formula of "a faith which seeks understanding" (*fides quaerens intellectum*) represents his attitude of mind. Firmly rooted in Christian tradition, and especially in Augustine, he sought to articulate his beliefs and to examine their sources, whether in pure reason or in divine revelation. As a theologian he will continue to be remembered for his treatise on the Redemption, the *Cur Deus Homo*; as a philosopher he expressed himself in the *Monologion* and the *Proslogion*. His view of man and the world, which is closely related to that of Augustine, need not detain us; his philosophical importance resides in what he has to say about the knowledge of God.

In the *Monologion* Anselm sets out lines of thought which are evidently in the ancestry of the Fourth Way of Aquinas. From the different degrees of value and of being observable in things about us he concludes to a *summum bonum* and a *summum ens* which is God. The point which obviously needs to be made clear in completion of an argument of this type is why such a supreme being should be supposed not only to be conceivable but actually to exist. Although there is no historical ground for supposing that Anselm was presented with this objection, he might well be understood as offering an answer to it in the ontological argument of the *Proslogion*.

His reasoning is as follows.[1] What we mean by God is a being than which nothing greater can be thought. Even the fool who, according to the Psalmist, says in his heart, There is no God, understands this meaning when he hears God spoken of. Therefore this being can

[1] *Proslogion*, cap. 2-4.

be said at least to have an existence as an object of thought. But to exist really as well as in the mind is to be greater than merely to exist in the mind. Hence, if the fool wants to say that God exists only as a figment of the mind, he is making God less than a similar being which would exist also in reality. That is, he is making God a being than which something greater can be thought, and so contradicting himself. Consequently, in order that God should genuinely be the being than which nothing greater can be thought, he must exist in reality as well as in the mind. God, then, really exists, and the fool, in denying this, is guilty of failing to understand what he is talking about.

This argument at once aroused interest and contradiction. Gaunilo, a monk of Marmoutiers, makes a brief appearance in the history of thought by voicing his objections in a work pleasantly entitled the Book on Behalf of the Fool (*Liber pro Insipiente*). He remarks in effect that the notion of a being than which nothing greater can be thought has no positive content; it is simply the notion of something beyond anything which we can positively conceive. But, even granted that this is a working idea of God, he says that an object as conceived has not a different content from the same object when we are aware of it as existing; it only has a different relation to our thinking faculty. Hence we cannot take a mental object and add existence to it. If we are to be aware of something as existing, it must be presented in the appropriate way to our minds as existing. Before we can say that the being than which nothing greater can be thought necessarily exists, we must have specific evidence that it in fact exists, and we cannot find this in its mere notion. Otherwise we might as well say that the most beautiful and fertile of all conceivable islands necessarily exists, or it would have less of excellence than any island which we know actually to exist. This is plainly futile, and so is Anselm's argument.

Anselm retorted by a *Liber Apologeticus contra Gaunilonem*, in which objection has stimulated him to make his position clearer. His argument, he says, does not apply to the most excellent of islands but to the most excellent of all beings, and to this being alone. We have a working notion of the being than which nothing greater can be thought, because we can understand what this means, and we have a working notion of existence too. Moreover, in this case, and in this case alone, we can see such a connection of ideas that it would be contradictory to suppose that the being than which nothing greater can be thought did not really exist. Thus the ontological argument takes clearer shape. What it amounts to is that infinite being, and infinite being alone, necessarily exists. It is enough to think of infinite being to see its necessary connection with existence. For all other things, since they are contingent, we require specific evidence in experience, or by reasoning from experience, in order to know that they exist. In the single case of God, the notion of God is sufficient to guarantee his existence. This is Anselm's famous and much discussed contribution to metaphysics.

§ 4

In the later middle ages the ontological argument proved on the whole acceptable to the Franciscan tradition. Among the Dominicans Albertus Magnus makes no final decision about it, but Aquinas firmly denies its validity. He remarks that, while God is in fact necessarily existent, we do not possess that insight into the divine nature which would enable us to perceive, as soon as we had a notion of God, that he existed. Existence does not strictly add anything to our *notion* of God; it rather transfers it from the ideal to the real order. Hence we require reasons based on experience, and not merely on an alleged conceptual necessity, in order that we may logically affirm the existence of God.[1]

Duns Scotus, on the other hand, thinks that Anselm's argument is valid if we make the explicit addition that the nature of God is not self-contradictory and is therefore intrinsically possible. This being given, it is true to say that a real thing is greater than a mere mental object, and so Anselm's conclusion follows.

The triangular relation of Anselm, Scotus and Aquinas is repeated in modern times with the terms replaced by Descartes, Leibniz and Kant. Descartes asserts the ontological argument in its simple form: the nature of infinite being is such that it must exist. Leibniz, like Scotus, maintains that this major premiss should be modified: if God is possible, he exists. Like Scotus too, he thinks that we are entitled to affirm the ideal possibility of the divine nature, so that the ontological argument in this shape is conclusive.

Kant objects that existence is not a real predicate or attribute. In a proposition which affirms existence of something, existence does not add another attribute to

[1] St. Thomas Aquinas: *Summa contra Gentiles,* lib. I, cap. 11, and *Summa Theologica* I, qu. 2, art. i.

the subject; it posits the subject as real, and that is the very assertion of the subject itself. If you deny existence of anything, you are not simply taking away a predicate from it; you are negating the whole subject. In these cases what you are really doing is to affirm or deny a relationship between your thought and fact. A hundred real dollars are not a larger sum than a hundred possible dollars; they differ as actual fact from the mere concept of such a thing. A proposition possesses ideal necessity when its denial involves a contradiction between subject and predicate, but the denial of the logical predicate of existence takes away the whole subject as well with all its predicates. Hence the denial of existence can never involve contradiction, and the ontological argument is invalid.[1]

The principle of the ontological argument is, then, that it is immediately evident that infinite being necessarily exists. It appears to be no more than an assertion that a relationship of entailment or implication holds between infinite being and necessary existence. But an entailment is a connection of the form: if there is A, there is B. Hence the principle can rightly be taken to mean only that, if there is an infinite being, it exists necessarily. With this expansion, however, it becomes quite clear that no light at all is thrown on the question whether an infinite being exists in fact or not. If the ontological argument were to have any bearing on the question whether an infinite being exists, it would have to become the assertion of a necessary connection between the thought of an infinite being and its existence:

[1] Kant: *Kritik der reinen Vernunft,* "Von der Unmöglichkeit eines ontologischen Beweises vom Dasein Gottes", A 592-602, B 620-30.

if an infinite being is thinkable, it exists. But it is
sufficiently evident that the mere fact that I can form a
concept of something can never by itself guarantee that
there is any reality corresponding with my thought.
Therefore, while it is true that, if an infinite being exists,
it exists necessarily, other grounds are required before an
infinite being can be asserted to exist in fact. With the
ontological argument alone, either the existence of
infinite being is assumed or the whole principle remains
in the purely conceptual sphere.

The error of the ontological argument is, as Kant says,
that it regards being as an attribute, whereas, if we are
to talk in terms of subject and attribute, everything else
might rather be said to be an attribute of being. Being
is presupposed to everything else which can be attributed
to any real thing. Anselm's mistake was, in effect, to
regard the universe as composed of a number of possible
things, some of which actually existed while others
remained merely possible. Merely possible things, however, have no reality in themselves; they have a kind of
reality only in the thought of those minds which think
them and in the power of those agents which can bring
them actually into being. Hence the ontological argument reposes upon a misunderstanding of the unique
character of the notion of existence. The positive sequel
of all this will appear in connection with Aquinas.

Nevertheless, although Anselm and his imitators were
mistaken in thinking that they had discovered a new
proof of the existence of God, they were perhaps strug-
gling to lay bare a principle which is of real importance
in the philosophical conception of God. For it is true,
and it is a cardinal point in Aquinas's own philosophy of

God, that necessary being can only be infinite being. As soon as it can be asserted that a necessary being exists, it follows that this is an infinite being. Kant thought that he had refuted this proposition by reducing it to the principle of the ontological argument. If all necessary being is infinite being, he says, it follows logically that some infinite being is necessary being. But, since there can be only one infinite being, it is possible in the consequent proposition to replace *some* infinite being by *all* infinite being. Hence the proposition that all necessary being is infinite being entails the proposition that all infinite being is necessary being, which is the principle of the ontological argument.

Kant is here guilty of a disastrous confusion of thought. He does not realize that what he has proved of the principle of the ontological argument is not that it is in every sense false but that it cannot serve as a foundation for asserting the existence of God. Since it is in reality true that, if there is an infinite being, it exists necessarily, the circumstance that this follows from the proposition that a necessary being can only be infinite being is no objection to the latter proposition. Hence, if you begin with the fact of experience that something exists and draw the obvious inference that, since it is impossible that everything should be dependent upon something else, there must be some necessary being, you can validly continue your line of thought by perceiving that this being must be infinite. Such an argument, beginning with the experience of existence, is no longer in the purely conceptual sphere. It is not, therefore, equivalent to the ontological argument, but it may not be unduly charitable to suppose that Anselm was glimpsing something of the kind, although he misinterpreted what he began to see and offered a process of reasoning which is formally invalid.

In spite, then, of the enormous difference in their general attitude and in their conclusions, it is not altogether out of place to deal in one chapter with Erigena and with Anselm. Erigena's neat ideal construction entirely neglects the import of individual existence; Anselm attempts to bring in the notion of existence but misuses it. The middle ages were not to evolve a satisfactory metaphysic until the nature of existence was better understood.

CHAPTER III

ABELARD AND THE TWELFTH CENTURY

§ 1

THE mediaeval thinkers were fortunate in having their attention called early to the problem of universals, for it is a problem whose ramifications extend over a great part of the philosophical field. A meditation on the nature of abstract thought leads insensibly to the consideration of the structure of fact in so far as it is intelligible or thinkable. Thus the problem of universals, as it presented itself to the mediaeval mind, served as an introduction to the whole range of philosophical logic and general metaphysics.

When I say of two roses that this is a rose and that is a rose, I am giving them the same name and using it in each case with the same meaning. It might seem that it could not have the same meaning unless in each case it meant the same *thing*. In that case, is there really one rose of which the particulars called by the name of rose are accidental modifications or manifestations? Or is that which is really the rose itself something apart from particular roses and belonging to a different order of being, so that through the perception of particular roses we glimpse a reality more absolute than the shifting objects of perceptual experience?

A more prosaic approach, however, enforces the realization that the two roses have no parts in common. The stalk and the petals and every other part of the flower are entirely distinct in the one and in the other.

All that they have in common may appear to be the name, or perhaps the concept, considered as a sign of its object. Are we to content ourselves with this nominalist view and to assert simply that the name or concept designates a certain group of objects, or any member of the group, without inquiring further why these objects group themselves in our minds as roses and those as lilies?

The latter question is too obvious and urgent to be left aside. Although two roses have no part, no *thing* in common, they could yet hardly be said to have nothing in common. They resemble each other, and if we can understand what resemblance means, we shall be able to grasp the nature of the universal concept. Two things would in ordinary language be said to resemble each other when they are partly the same and partly different. This cannot mean, as we have already seen, that they have a part which is the same and a part which is different; there is no concrete reality belonging in common to both. But there is resemblance where there is identity in difference, where the identity and the difference are in reality inseparable although distinguishable by thought. A good deal more could evidently be said about the problem of universals, but this will serve to make intelligible the vacillations of the earlier mediaeval thinkers in dealing with the question.

§ 2

The celebrated passage of Porphyry which aroused the attention of the mediaevals is one in which that philosopher raises certain questions about universals

without venturing to provide answers. He asks whether
genera and species are real or merely figments of the
mind, whether, if they are real, they are corporeal or
incorporeal, and whether their reality resides in the
sensible things which are members of the genus or species
or is something distinct from these. The mediaeval
thinkers might have found the Aristotelian solution of
these difficulties in Boethius, for Boethius says clearly
enough that genera and species are real but have their
reality in their members; although their members may
be perceptible through the senses, the apprehension of
universals requires more than perception; it requires
comparison and abstraction, for a universal is a resemblance cognized by thought (*similitudo cogitata*). It
does not, however, appear to have been noticed that
Boethius provided the essential answer, for Godfrey of
St. Victor, in a well-known piece of twelfth-century
academic light verse, represents him as embarrassed by
the differences of learned opinion and unable to make
up his mind which side to take in settling the question.

Assidet Boethius stupens de hac lite,
Audiens quid hic et hic afferat perite,
Et quid cui faveat non discernit rite,
Nec praesumit solvere litem definite.

The earliest mediaeval speculation manifests a realism
untempered by any more subtle consideration. To know
is to know something; since thinking employs universal
terms, universals must themselves be real. The principle
seems almost to have been: one word, one thing.
In the Carolingian age Fridugise of Tours, writing

De Nihilo et Tenebris, delighted in the paradox of attributing a certain reality to nothingness and to darkness on the ground that they were significant terms of thought.

The first reaction, when it came, was equally extreme. Just as the original realism had been based too exclusively on the true principle of the objectivity of knowledge, so the new view was based too exclusively on the true principle that only the individual is real. The authorship of opposition to realism is usually assigned to Roscellinus towards the end of the eleventh century. Since the individual alone is real, universality belongs only to the words by which we designate indifferently one or other member of a class of individuals; a universal term is *flatus vocis*. It obviously did not occur to Roscellinus that the same problem can be raised about words as about things. Each instance of the use of a word is itself a different thing, a different sound or a different mark on paper; how then do we come to speak of instances of the *same* word? Apart from this, how did Roscellinus explain the manner in which we group things under the same name? Why do we call roses by the name of *rose*, and not lilies? Our information about him is too scanty to enable us to answer these questions of interpretation. Henceforward, at any rate, those who dealt with logic from the viewpoint of language, *secundum vocem*, were opposed to those who dealt with it from the viewpoint of reality, *secundum rem*. Everything invited to the formation of a synthesis which should do justice to both points of view, but this did not come at once.

Meanwhile, for example, we find Odo of Tournai

defending the traditional realistic logic against the pernicious novelties of the nominalist Raimbert of Lille, and maintaining that humanity is one reality manifested in ever-changing forms throughout the generations of men. With more elaborate argument the ancient realism is defended by William of Champeaux, who died as bishop of Châlons in 1120. William, however, was fated to have Abelard among his students and, under the pressure of the young logician's objections, had gradually to modify his views. Having given up the theory that a universal is essentially one thing of which the individuals which are members of the class are merely accidental modifications, he first subscribed to the vague formula that there is a certain unity of indifference in the members of a class, and finally contented himself with saying that there is no identity but only likeness.

A considerable number of theories aiming at compromise appear in the early part of the twelfth century, but most of them are regrettably vague. Adelard of Bath speaks of different aspects (*respectus*) under which a thing can be considered as this individual, as belonging to a species and as belonging to a genus. Walter of Mortagne, using the term *status*, seems to intend very much the same as Adelard. Jocelin of Soissons prefers to look at the question in extension and says that universality belongs to the whole collection or class, while individuality characterizes its members. These views are catalogued in the *Metalogicon* of John of Salisbury, and are evidently attempts to reconcile the objectivity of knowledge with the primary reality of the individual.

For a precise and accurate treatment, however, we

have to go to the logical writings of Peter Abelard himself. Abelard sets out from the now established position that reality belongs primarily to the individual. Specific and generic names, however, are common to classes of individuals, but the universal is not merely a name, for it is significantly predicated of the class of individuals to which it applies. It signifies a real property of the individual subject, although it places this in an isolation which does not belong to it outside the mind. The formation of the universal concept must be referred to the abstractive activity of thought; in this way it can be true both that its whole content is real and that its form of universality is a mental product. "When I consider this man merely as a substance or body, and not also as an animal or man or grammarian, I am thinking of nothing which does not belong to him but I am not considering everything which belongs to him. . . . One factor is thought of separately from another but not as separate from it" (*Separatim namque haec res ab alia, non separata intelligitur*). This is the classical mediaeval solution of the problem of universals, and, when it had sunk into men's minds, there was no further controversy on the subject until after the age of Aquinas, when Duns Scotus raised new metaphysical questions about the structure which fact must possess in order that abstract thought may be possible, and when William of Ockham, proceeding in the opposite direction, founded a new type of nominalism.

§ 3

His solution of the problem of universals was Abelard's chief departmental contribution to philosophy, but his personality and spirit exercised a wide general influence on the development of thought in the twelfth century. His stormy career gave a new intellectual impetus to his own and the succeeding generation. The trouble with him, of course, was that not only could he not suffer fools gladly but he could not even suffer wise men gladly if their wisdom was of a different stamp from his own. Yet, in spite of his defects, he remains a fascinating personality, and we are fortunate in possessing his own account of the greater part of his life in the long letter which is usually known as the *Historia Calamitatum*.

Born at Le Pallet near Nantes in 1079, the eldest son of a knightly family, Abelard renounced his feudal rights in order to follow a career of learning. After being initiated into dialectic by Roscellinus, he made himself obnoxious to William of Champeaux by presenting him with unanswerable objections, and soon set up as a teacher on his own account. The established masters made things difficult for the pert young newcomer, who was ready to treat anyone as he had treated William, and he went off to become a student again, but this time of theology. The teacher he chose was Anselm of Laon, the most celebrated theologian of the period, but Abelard found him disappointing and, forgetful of how much trouble he had stirred up for himself by his tactless handling of William of Champeaux, he behaved in the same way to Anselm. He announced a rival lecture on the interpretation of Ezekiel and found himself greeted as a new master of theology. This, obviously, was not pleasing to Anselm, and Abelard had to leave Laon and return to Paris, a teacher now of theology in place of dialectic.

It was at this period that he fell in with Héloïse, the niece of the canon Fulbert with whom he lodged. Their genuinely tragic connection deserves something better than the rather sugary sentimentality which has often been lavished upon it. Abelard candidly describes how, beginning by teaching her in his spare time, he ended by falling in love with her. When their son Astrolabius was born, he wanted to marry her, although this would of course have ended his career as a cleric, and her unselfish arguments in opposition have a curiously twentieth-century ring. "Could anyone intent on theological or philosophical meditations", she said, "put up with the cries of children, the foolishness of nurses hushing them and the tumult of a household full of men and women? Could he tolerate babies with their continual dirtiness? It is all right for the rich, who have plenty of room in their palaces or mansions and whose wealth makes them superior to expenses and daily worries. But philosophers are not in the same position as the rich, nor do those who are amassing wealth and engrossed by worldly cares give much time to theology or philosophy." In the end, however, Abelard prevailed, and the marriage took place secretly. But the relations of Héloïse seem to have suspected that he was unwilling to acknowledge her publicly as his wife and took their cruel revenge upon him.

In an emotional reaction from this shock Abelard became a monk at Saint Denis, while Héloïse took the veil at Argenteuil. Meanwhile some of his theological opinions became a subject of complaint, and he was condemned to burn his book *De Unitate et Trinitate Divina* by a synod held at Soissons in 1121. Finding his monastery intolerable, he adopted a solitary life in the place where he built the oratory of the Paraclete, but students soon flocked to him again. Fearing that theological teaching would get him into trouble once more, he handed over the Paraclete to Héloïse and her nuns, and consented to become abbot of St. Gildas in his native land of Brittany. Here he was unlucky as usual; the abbey turned out to be in so relaxed a state of discipline that he could do nothing with it. He returned first to the Paraclete and then to the Mont Sainte Geneviève at Paris, where he resumed his teaching of theology. This merely procured him a new condemnation by a synod at Sens in 1140, whose decisions were confirmed by Pope Innocent II. He submitted and took refuge with his friend Peter the Venerable, abbot of Cluny, under whose protection he died in 1142.

There can be no doubt that Abelard made mistakes. He was a pioneer in the analytic speculative theology which is so characteristic a product of the middle ages, and he never seems to have been quite clear about the respective parts of faith and of reason. His scornful and intolerant character made it impossible for him to come to an agreement with men like St. Bernard, whose sanctity and fundamental rightness he overlooked and whose lack of formal intellectual training he despised. Yet Abelard's own intentions were fundamentally sound; he was only trying to develop more completely and more systematically the faith seeking understanding which St. Anselm had cherished. The character which could deserve the affection and respect shown by Peter of

Cluny for Abelard in the letter to Héloïse which tells her of his death, and is surely one of the most moving of mediaeval documents, cannot be lightly condemned. Other men, his successors in the twelfth and thirteenth centuries, not excluding Thomas Aquinas and Duns Scotus, were to walk more discreetly and more securely in his footsteps, but we should not forget to pay tribute to the pioneering work of Abelard and to the impulse which it gave to later speculation in spite of its blemishes.

In the circumstances of his life it is not surprising that Abelard's works remain somewhat fragmentary. In pure philosophy, apart from his logical works, the glosses on Porphyry, on the *Categories* and on the *De Interpretatione* of Aristotle, he left an ethical treatise, the *Scito Te Ipsum.* Here he displays an appreciation of the subjective factor in conduct, of the importance of viewpoint and intention, which is almost unique in the middle ages. But he left still more, in spite of all his faults, an example of genuine devotion to the intellectual life, and for this his very faults and the misfortunes which they brought upon him only increase the duty of acknowledging his real merits.

§ 4

The twelfth century was not to produce a great systematic philosopher, but it was marked by a series of respectable scholars and thinkers. The abbey of St. Victor at Paris, in which William of Champeaux had passed some years before he became a bishop, was an important centre of study. The German Hugh of St. Victor (1096-1141) was its most distinguished figure.

While he holds a considerable place in the history of theology, in philosophy he was something of an eclectic. His view of universals was derived from Abelard; he adopted an atomic account of the material world; his psychology was based on Augustine; for the way to God he relied chiefly upon an inference from the finite and temporal character of the self as given to consciousness. His work was carried on in the next generation by the Scotsman Richard of St. Victor. The other well-known name connected with St. Victor, that of Adam, the author of an immense number of not unpleasing doggerel Latin hymns, does not appear in the history of philosophy.

Chartres was an even greater intellectual centre for part of the twelfth century. It was specially noted for its humanistic and literary interests, and a good deal of work was done in the physical sciences, especially by William of Conches, who professed a more developed atomic theory than that of Hugh of St. Victor. The philosophers, Bernard and Thierry of Chartres, were Platonists, and their systems can be rapidly described as a commentary on the *Timaeus* with the addition of Neoplatonic and Augustinian elements. Gilbert de la Porrée (1076-1154), however, who taught at Chartres before becoming bishop of Poitiers, was more of an Aristotelian; his *Liber Sex Principiorum*, in which he endeavoured to supplement the *Categories* of Aristotle, became a classic of mediaeval logic and was studied for centuries in conjunction with the *Organon* itself.

The Englishman John of Salisbury died as bishop of Chartres in 1180. He had been a disciple of Abelard, of William of Conches and of Gilbert de la Porée, and gives a pleasant picture of his student days at Paris and Chartres, making the comment when he returned later on to the scenes of his youth that the same problems were still being heatedly discussed with the same arguments, and no one seemed to have got any farther. Later he was for twenty years on the archiepiscopal staff at Canterbury under Theobald and St. Thomas à Becket. An old chronicle provides one of those revelations of character which make history come to life, in the account which it gives of his remonstrance to Becket for being so unconciliatory in his first interview with the knights who eventually murdered him. "We all have to die," the archbishop replied, "nor should be diverted from the right way by the fear of death; I am more ready to undergo death for the sake of God and of justice than they to inflict it." "We," rejoined John, "are sinners and not yet prepared to die; I see no one here who wishes to die for dying's sake but you." [1]

John of Salisbury was more of a scholar and an eclectic than an original philosopher. The *Policraticus* is a discursive work concerned with political theory and incidentally enumerating the systems of philosophy known to John. The *Metalogicon* is a plea for the study of logic; it contains an account of the different contemporary views on universals and solves the question more or less in the spirit of Abelard. It is important, too, as containing an analysis of the *Organon* of Aristotle, which was just then coming once more to be known in its entirety.

Alan of Lille was another great scholar of the twelfth century, but his philosophy, too, was eclectic rather

[1] Cit. and trans. by C. C. J. Webb: *John of Salisbury*, p. 117.

than original. The thinkers of the period are of mainly historical interest, but they prepared the way for the major developments of the thirteenth century. Meanwhile Aristotle was being rediscovered and universities were taking definite shape, so that we can see a great difference in the state of learning in 1100 and in 1200, and it is not inappropriate to speak of a twelfth-century renaissance.

§ 5

Universities are a mediaeval creation. In the early middle ages the schools, which were usually attached to cathedrals or monasteries, had little organization or continuity. When good teachers were available, they flourished, but in a few years they might be almost deserted. In the twelfth century itself we see how a brilliant group of scholars brought Chartres into a temporary celebrity which in a short time was completely eclipsed. From the writings of Abelard and John of Salisbury it appears that anyone might set up as a teacher at Paris if he could collect an audience.

With the new enthusiasm for learning and the great increase in the number of students, it was natural that measures of organization should gradually be introduced. The development was in fact gradual; it is impossible to assign a date of foundation to the first mediaeval universities. The charters which they eventually received were a recognition of an already existing state of affairs; the faculties had begun to be organized, and masters and scholars formed a self-governing unity. The earliest university is usually said to be Bologna, but it was always predominantly a law school. The greatest of mediaeval universities was indisputably Paris. At the time of Abelard there were the three schools of Notre Dame, St. Victor and the Mont Sainte Geneviève; by the end of the twelfth century these had coalesced into the university which received a charter from Philip Augustus in 1200 and a papal privilege in 1231. Oxford was growing up at the same time; the origin of Cambridge can be more exactly dated by a migration from Oxford in 1209.

The teaching of philosophy was in the mediaeval university associated both with the arts and with theology. Dialectic or logic acquired a dominant position among the arts, while the treatment of metaphysical and ethical questions fell to the masters of theology. That is why we have, for example, to look for a great part of Aquinas's philosophy in his professedly theological works, such as the *Summa Theologica*. But, in spite of this mingling of philosophy and theology in practice, it is evident when we read the great men of the thirteenth century that they were very well aware of what was philosophy and what theology, what fell within the province of pure reason and what presupposed revelation. With the rediscovery of Aristotle, the reading of his works gained a greater place for pure philosophy and for questions which we should now consider to belong to the physical sciences.

With the paucity and dearness of books before the invention of printing, oral teaching was of primary importance. The tradition of lecturing has perhaps even now failed to take full account of the change of conditions brought about by printing; while lectures remain useful for general introduction, bibliographical direction and the emphasizing of salient points, it is not always recognized that an intelligent student can acquire information by reading in half the time that it would take to assimilate it through the ear. In the middle ages, however, lectures were inevitably the chief means of instruction, and they were supplemented by disputations in which the students themselves took part.

The nature of mediaeval teaching dictated the form of mediaeval writing. The lecture, *lectio*, a reading, took the form of commentary on some accepted textbook, but it was a commentary which often diverged considerably, in accordance with the taste of the lecturer, from the opinions and even the subject-matter of the author commented upon. Although the authority of Aristotle was very great in the middle ages, the commentaries upon his works are by no means slavish. The mediaeval convention, of course, was to seek agreement, and even sometimes to assume it when it was fairly patently not there, and this tends to obscure the originality of mediaeval writers when examined by the modern reader, now that Professor A tends usually to stress his divergences from Professor B, and anything but the latest new theory is commonly considered rather dull. But, under the bland mediaeval assumption that Aristotle or some other great authority is being explained, he is in fact often being considerably modified. At the same time the mediaeval thinkers were not ashamed to profess agreement when they did agree, and it was thought sufficient originality to present the old truth with new force. This panegyric is fully applicable to the creative period of the middle ages; it should be acknowledged equally that in the decline of scholasticism opinions did become fatiguingly stereotyped.

The accepted author in theology was Peter Lombard, who taught in Paris and became its bishop in the middle of the twelfth century. A large proportion of mediaeval philosophy, as well as theology, is to be found in the innumerable commentaries on the four books of the *Sentences* of Peter Lombard. Besides these there were the records of disputations and studies of special questions treated in the form of disputation, whether the continuous exposition of the ordinary *quaestiones disputatae* or the more miscellaneous *quaestiones quodlibetales*. Short *opuscula* dealt with particular problems in more familiar literary form, and there were a certain number of larger original constructions, especially the *summae theologicae*, of which that of St. Thomas is so famous. In this way mediaeval writing clearly bears the stamp of the teaching methods of the universities.

The twelfth century was a period of preparation. The urge to study grew, the knowledge of the past was once again brought to bear, and universities were formed. Its most important contribution to the new life of philosophy in the thirteenth century, the recovery of Aristotle, has been alluded to but remains to be studied in some detail.

CHAPTER IV

THE RECOVERY OF ARISTOTLE

§ 1

FOR us, nowadays, Aristotle is a philosopher, and still perhaps the greatest name in the history of philosophy, but until three centuries ago he was more even than that; his work covered the whole range of the natural sciences, and he was considered a grave authority there as well. His systematic scientific conceptions have been superseded, although he is still reckoned to have been an accurate observer. For us his philosophical fame alone remains, but we shall not appreciate his significance for the mediaeval thinkers unless we recapture the idea of him as the master of those who know in every field of human speculation. The recovery of Aristotle was for the middle ages the acquisition not only of a philosophical system but of a whole encyclopaedia of scientific knowledge. To the men of that time he appeared almost as a personification of the human reason which they sought to integrate with the divine revelation acknowledged by them in Christian tradition.

When barbarism descended on western Europe, his works, with the exception of the elements of his logic, were forgotten. They were preserved by the Byzantines, and there continued to be Byzantine commentators on Aristotle. Nevertheless, the Byzantine was a static civilization with no very vigorous interest in philosophical thought. In an excessively dynamic age like the present, it is not for us to scorn the merits of a static

56

civilization, but the fact remains that the Byzantines, while preserving the treasures of the Greek past, made comparatively little use of them.

Aristotelianism came back to life again when brought into contact with the new and virile Mohammedan movement. Mohammedanism is essentially a rather simple and unintellectual religion, and it seems at first sight strange that it should have given new life to philosophy. Yet speculation is a natural human activity, and, whenever the human spirit is deeply stirred, it tends to express itself in more ways than the one from which the first stimulus came. There was always, however, a conflict between the orthodox Mohammedan theologians and the independent-minded philosophers, and the conflict ended with the victory of the former, but not before a series of important Arabic philosophers had developed systems arising from the contact of their Mohammedan tradition with Aristotelianism and with Neoplatonism.

Geographically the Arabic thinkers are distributed into two groups, an earlier group belonging to Baghdad and a later one to Spain. Of the Baghdad group, apart from Alfarabi, who is a link in the transmission of Aristotle's proof of the existence of God as the unmoved mover, the most important is Avicenna (Ibn Sina, 980-1037). He employed the arguments from contingency and from causation to reach the existence of God, and his method of presenting them had an influence which is traceable in the corresponding ways of St. Thomas. Matter he regarded, like Aristotle, as eternal and uncreated. Given these two extremes, the supreme intelligence of God and the complete indeterminacy of matter, the systematic construction of Avicenna's philosophy consists in a description of the emanation from God of subordinate intelligences which are at the same time the source of determination and form in the material world. The higher intelligences are brought into connection with the astronomy of the time; they are the intelligences of the heavenly spheres. The lowest pure intelligence is the active intellect which governs the sublunary or terrestrial world.

Aristotle had distinguished two aspects of human thinking, the active and the passive. The passive intellect was the mind as receptive of concepts from the world of experience; the active intellect was the power of abstraction and of original thinking. Sometimes it seems almost as if these were not merely two functions of the mind but two intellects, and in an enigmatic passage Aristotle speaks of the active intellect as essentially separate or separable from matter and alone immortal and perpetual.[1] If by χωριστὸς he means separable, his view harmonizes with individual immortality; if he means that the active intellect is something essentially separate and apart from matter, it might appear to be a pure intelligence distinct from the individual human mind. Then the active intellect might be identified with God, as by Alexander of Aphrodisias, or with some subordinate but still superhuman intelligence. This latter interpretation was current among the Arabs, and it was, as we have just seen, the opinion of Avicenna, who assigned to the active intellect the function not only of actuating human thought but also of exercising causal

[1] Aristotle: *De Anima* III, 5, 430a.

determination upon the whole process of events on the earth.

In spite of his use of the Neoplatonic concept of emanation instead of creation, Avicenna is not to be pantheistically interpreted; the intelligences are adequately distinct from one another. Nor did his theory of the single active intellect prevent him from asserting the immortality of individual human minds. An illumination from the active intellect is needed in order that they should actually think, but their existence is independent of matter. Hence there was much in Avicenna with which Christians could sympathize, and, when he came to the notice of the scholastics, he was on the whole a welcome discovery.

Algazel (1058-1111) was the most notable representative of the theological reaction against the relatively independent philosophical thinking of men like Avicenna. He remained a speculative theologian and a speculative mystic of interest, but his speculation was thoroughly subordinated to the teaching of the Koran. From his time onwards the centre of philosophical gravity in the Arab world shifted from Baghdad towards the West.

The greatest of the Arabic philosophers in Spain was Averroes (Ibn Roschd, 1126-98). Like Avicenna he maintained the emanation from God of the intelligences which governed the heavenly spheres, but unlike his predecessor he held that they emanated not one from the other but all directly and eternally from God. Matter, according to him too, is equally eternal and must be conceived as possessing an active tendency towards the forms which are educed from it, rather than imposed upon it, under the influence of the intelligences. The lowest of the pure intelligences is that of the moon, which is at the same time the active intellect presiding over human thinking. The individual human mind, with its passive intellect or receptive function, is inseparable from the body and perishes with it; the single active intellect is alone immortal. Such a theory is no more in accordance with the Koran than it is with Christian teaching, and Averroes resorted to an allegorical interpretation of the Mohammedan faith; he had in fact nothing to learn from the Christian modernist of to-day in the way of expedients for making the best of both worlds. In his own day, however, his assertions of the eternity of the world and of the uncreatedness of matter, of the unity of the intellect and the perishable character of the individual soul, raised problems which were to be hotly debated by the Christian Aristotelians of the thirteenth century. For his prestige was very great; just as Aristotle came to be called the Philosopher *par excellence,* so Averroes was known as the Commentator.

The heterodoxy of the views of Averroes was too much for the Mohammedans and contributed to the discredit of philosophy among them, but there were still Jewish philosophers in the Arab dominions. Already in the eleventh century Avencebrol (Solomon ibn Gebirol) had put forward an emanation theory in which the supreme being, beyond mind as beyond matter, recalls the One of Plotinus. Minds, like material things, are composed of matter and form, but of a spiritual matter and a spiritual form. Hence matter is no longer the principle of pure potentiality which it was for Aristotle, but a principle of specific potentiality which differs in different things. There are various kinds of matter as there are various kinds of form.

Moses Maimonides (1135-1204), frequently alluded to by the Latin scholastics as Rabbi Moses, has a system which is closer in spirit to theirs. His proofs of the existence of God by motion, by causality and by contingency had an evident influence on the later presentation of similar lines of thought by St. Thomas in the first three of the Five Ways. The world is temporal and created by God. In his disquisitions on the nature of God, Maimonides, in consonance with the Jewish tradition of an absolute divine transcendence, has a certain agnostic tendency and insists on the way of negation. We strictly know of God not what he is but what he is not, for all the objects of experience are finite and clogged with potentiality, whereas God is the somewhat beyond all potentiality and limitation. Here the balance was to be redressed by Aquinas and others like him.

The sum total of all this is that the Arabs and Jews had revived an Aristotelianism often strongly tinged with Neoplatonism. They had related their philosophical researches to a theological tradition, whether Jewish or Mohammedan. When Latin Europe came into contact with their work, the recovery of the text of Aristotle and the theories of these Arabic and Jewish thinkers were to present new questions for discussion and to stimulate a much more elaborate philosophical inquiry than mediaeval Christian civilization had hitherto known. The new philosophy had also to be adjusted to the Christian faith, so that the thinkers of the thirteenth century had to rise to a great occasion, and they did so.

§ 2

The principal places in which the Latin West came into contact with Arab civilization were Spain and Sicily. In these countries especially, we can trace the development of the new learning by the translations made in the course of the twelfth and thirteenth centuries, translations of Aristotle and of two dialogues of Plato, and of the newer philosophers and commentators. It is important to realize that it was not until the Renaissance that the Greek text of Aristotle was commonly studied; the mediaeval thinkers made acquaintance with him in Latin versions, sometimes even at first in versions taken from the Arabic translations and therefore at third hand. It is remarkable that they were able, in general, to understand him so accurately.

The whole of the *Organon* became accessible in the version of a certain James of Venice quite early in the twelfth century. In the middle of the century the pleasantly named Henry Aristippus, archdeacon of Catania, produced a translation of the fourth book of the *Meteorologica*. He was also the translator of the *Phaedo* and *Meno* of Plato, which were now added to the *Timaeus*, already known in the West, but received much less attention than the growing versions of Aristotle.

Meanwhile there was a whole group of translators in Spain, aided by the patronage of Raymond, archbishop of Toledo. These included Gerard of Cremona and Dominic Gundissalvi, who worked from the Arabic and introduced many Arabic philosophical and scientific works to the knowledge of the Latins. From this group came, as far as Aristotle is concerned, versions of the

Physics, the *Posterior Analytics, De Caelo et Mundo, De Generatione et Corruptione* and the first three books of the *Meteorologica.* Later, in Spain too, Michael Scot translated the *Historia Animalium, De Partibus Animalium* and *De Generatione Animalium.*

Versions of Aristotle were already being made directly from the Greek towards the end of the twelfth century, and these are presumably more important, but their authorship is still a matter of historical investigation. In the thirteenth century Robert Grosseteste, bishop of Lincoln, translated the *Nicomachean Ethics,* adding both notes of his own and renderings of some of the former commentators. Finally, with the encouragement of St. Thomas, William of Moerbeke, partly making new translations and partly revising the old ones, produced in the middle of the thirteenth century what was to be the standard mediaeval Latin version of Aristotle. The result is a strangely rugged work, so literal that it is easy to reconstruct the Greek text which was employed but, in its literalness, by no means easy to understand by itself. Nevertheless it sufficed as a foundation for the mighty edifice of Aristotelian scholasticism, although probably its difficulty deterred any but the most persevering students from reading much of Aristotle himself and made the majority see him largely through the eyes of his scholastic commentators.

§ 3

That the doctrines of Aristotle were currently taught in the university of Paris at the beginning of the thirteenth century appears from their becoming the object of ecclesiastical prohibition, first on the part of local authority and later from the papacy itself. Theories such as those of the eternity of the world and of the unity of the human intellect, which had been emphasized by some of the Arab thinkers, were evidently the cause of this intervention. But these measures of the Church turned out to be a delaying action rather than a fully mounted counter-offensive. In 1231 Gregory IX set up a commission of three theologians to consider what corrections were necessary to make Aristotle acceptable. Although this commission does not seem to have performed its allotted task, the adaption of Aristotle was in fact carried out gradually and comparatively peacefully, and by the middle of the century studies were firmly established on Aristotelian lines. Some teachers were more explicitly Aristotelian, others harked back more to the philosophy of Augustine, but none were completely immune from the new influence.

There is already a great deal of Aristotelianism in the works of William of Auvergne, bishop of Paris (d. 1249). The chief part, however, in the intellectual movement of the thirteenth century was to be taken by the new orders of friars, Dominican and Franciscan. After some hesitation on their own part about whether this was their proper work and some reluctance on the part of the universities to admit them, the Dominicans and Franciscans were soon taking a dominant share in the work of the universities. The first great Franciscan master at Paris was the Englishman Alexander of Hales (d. 1245), whose *Summa Theologica*, on its philosophical side, was an attempted synthesis of Augustine and Aristotle. The leading representative of the Dominicans was St. Albert

the Great (1193 or 1207-80), who in the course of his
long life taught at several places in Germany as well as
at Paris and had among his pupils St. Thomas Aquinas.
Albertus Magnus was a scholar of monumental learning
and an extremely prolific writer; if he did not himself
succeed in producing a coherent system from Augustine
and the earlier scholastics, Aristotle, the Neoplatonists
and the Arabs, he at any rate amassed the materials for
it and thereby prepared the way for St. Thomas.

We should not have a clear idea of the intellectual
situation in the thirteenth century unless we took into
account the opposition movement which tended to see
Aristotle through the interpretation of Averroes and
consequently to put forward theories incompatible with
Christianity. The leader of the Paris Averroists was
Siger of Brabant. They maintained, as philosophical
truth, that the world was eternal and necessarily produced by God, that causal necessitation so penetrated the
world that there was no room for the freedom of the
human will, and that there was only one immaterial
human intellect or soul, so that individual personality
perished at death. They endeavoured to keep themselves on the right side of ecclesiastical authority by the
somewhat enigmatic doctrine of the two truths: what was
true in philosophy might be false in theology. They can
scarcely have meant to affirm this doctrine literally;
neither their contemporaries could, nor can we ourselves,
easily avoid the suspicion that their preferences went to
what they thought to be philosophical truth. Perhaps,
like Averroes, they really meant that while philosophy
yielded plain unvarnished truth, religious tradition,
when opposed in its obvious sense to philosophy, could

be given a certain value by means of symbolic or allegorical interpretation. At any rate this subterfuge did not avail them much, and a part of the work of the orthodox scholastics was to demolish their reasoning. For by this time St. Bonaventure and St. Thomas were in full activity, and the greatest period of mediaeval thought had begun.

Meanwhile Aristotelian studies had been making their way at Oxford too, with the help and encouragement of Grosseteste. Grosseteste was scientist as well as philosopher and theologian, and his application of mathematical methods to physical questions foreshadows the developments of modern times. The notion of light as the primary attribute of body, derived from Neoplatonic sources and embraced by many of the earlier mediaeval thinkers, receives special emphasis from Grosseteste. The Franciscans, whom he aided to settle at Oxford, were very active there in the thirteenth century, producing thinkers such as Adam Marsh and Thomas of York. They produced also that heroic misfit Roger Bacon, a difficult character, no doubt, but one who scarcely deserved the long incarceration with which his turbulence was requited. His insistence on experimental methods and his own experimental researches have earned him the respect of later ages, but these activities lay outside the main mediaeval line of interest, and the men of his time could not foresee how fruitful they would eventually turn out to be. What was noticed by them and, in modern phrase, put their backs up was a series of violent attacks on most of the leading lights of the period. In strict philosophy Bacon really derived more from the earlier scholastics than from the new Aristotelian movement, but he was not an opponent of Aristotle; he maintained rather that everyone else misunderstood Aristotle, and declared his desire to incinerate all the translations hitherto made. In short, by the middle of the thirteenth century, Aristotle, however interpreted and however modified, had come to stay; the history of mediaeval thought was now to be the history of Aristotelian scholasticism.

§ 4

At a later period a rigid adherence to the details of Aristotelian physics was an obstacle to the development of modern science; on this account it must all the more be stressed that the introduction of Aristotelianism in the thirteenth century was a powerful reinforcement of the genuine scientific spirit, of the spirit of exact and dispassionate observation of what things are and how they behave. The superficial religious mind tends to disparage created things and thinks that thereby it does honour to their Creator. Some versions of Platonism strengthen this tendency with their view of the world of experience as a mere shadow of the world of essences, which, for Christian Platonism, was the Divine Word. The new Aristotelianism was a reminder that the things of experience had a being and an activity of their own, and deserved to be looked at for their own sake. The Christian Aristotelians were not slow to point out that it did more honour to God to recognize that he had created a world with its own value and interest than to suppose that men were expected to keep their gaze averted from it. In this way a sound religious philosophy was an encouragement to the spirit of humanism and of scientific investigation. Aristotelianism brought with it the full acknowledgment of the dependence of human knowledge upon sensation. Sense-experience was no longer regarded as a mere jumping-off ground from which the mind leapt to higher things; it was recognized to provide the material from which thought elaborated even its most ethereal concepts. Human thought began with abstraction from the data of sensation; the intellect, having no innate ideas prior to sensation, had to be passive or receptive of concepts from experience, but it was at the same time active in raising to intelligibility by abstraction the matter provided for it by the senses. When concepts were formed, the intellect could perceive relations between them and so attain to first principles. Deductive logic, by the application of principles to specific classes of things and ultimately to the individual things of experience, was the means by which knowledge could be amplified. The more complex, less certain but nevertheless very fruitful procedure of inductive logic was scarcely glimpsed by the mediaeval Aristotelians; that is of course why, in spite of the possession of a genuine scientific spirit, the middle ages made so little progress in those sciences whose methods we now know as having to be experimental and hypothetical. On the other side of the account, where deductive logic was in place, the mediaeval thinkers displayed exceptional acumen and reached memorable results.

The explanation in detail of the process of knowledge was an elaborate commentary upon Aristotle's statement that knowledge was a reception of form (*species*) without matter. The sense-object was known through the reception of the *species sensibilis*; the *species* was not itself an object of knowledge except to further reflection, but was that through which the object came to be known. Similarly, intellectual abstraction was described as the formation of a *species intelligibilis*. Later scholasticism distinguished formally between the *species impressa*, which preceded and stimulated the cognitive act, and the *species expressa*, which was either the cognitive act itself or something brought into existence by it, an image or concept for future reference. In spite of the unanimity of language, there was considerable divergence in its interpretation, and we have here, as with other doctrines, to think twice before fathering upon the more flexible thinkers of the thirteenth century the systematic classifications of their later followers.

The primary reality of the individual existent was at the base of Aristotelian metaphysics. While the metaphysical dissection of reality was made in terms of the Aristotelian categories of substance and accident, substance was not the inert substratum to which it was reduced by Locke but the active principle from which attributes and activities sprang. The real unity of a thing in spite of its metaphysical stratification was explained by the equally Aristotelian distinction of potentiality and actuality. The subject was a potency in relation to its attributes as a whole, and some of its attributes were potencies in relation to others. The tension of potency and act was to be found even in substance itself and constituted metaphysical composition; only God was metaphysically simple and pure act without any admixture of potentiality. An adequate explanation of things involved reference to the four causes enumerated by Aristotle, material, formal, efficient and final. Aristotelian metaphysics, however, have curiously little to say about the notion of being; it was here especially that the mediaeval thinkers, inspired by reflection on the Christian conception of God, broke new ground.

God, known through creatures as the uncaused in relation to the caused and the necessary in relation to the contingent, must be pure act and pure being. St. Thomas, more than anyone else, makes clear how the divine attributes follow from the notion of pure being, *ipsum esse*. The Christian Aristotelians, in contrast with some of their Arab precursors, had to show too that the creation of the world was an act of free choice and that it either had to be or at any rate could be a beginning in time. On these questions, as we have already mentioned, many of the controversies of the thirteenth century turned.

The material world was interpreted in terms of matter and form. Here again there was opposition between the more metaphysical conception of *materia prima* as a completely indeterminate substratum and the more physical theory of it as exhibiting the generic character of body with some, however poor, reality and determination of its own. The Aristotelian theory of the soul as the form of the human body linked psychology with physics. The soul was a separable form, but it was naturally destined to a physical organism and in some sense incomplete without it; the body, then, was not an encumbrance but deserved respect as a part of the essential man. Thought entailed free will and responsibility, but it may be said that the analysis of free will was not carried as far in the middle ages as we might have expected; while deliberation and choice were analysed, the conditions under which choice is in the full sense free were not examined very narrowly.

The systematic treatment of ethics was governed by the Aristotelian notion of end or purpose, but eudaemonism was given a new meaning when it ceased to be merely an egocentric development of the individual and became his attainment of an end beyond himself in the enjoyment of God. This adaptation of the *Nicomachean Ethics* to a religious view of life may be studied especially in the *Prima Secundae* of St. Thomas. The emphasis on man as being made by God and for God, and finding his deepest life in his relationship to God, brought with it also an emancipation from the old Greek totalitarianism. Since the state could certainly not dictate to its citizens on the profoundest issues of all, men began to ask more explicitly what were the due limitations of political authority. In the middle ages we find, therefore, the first explicit formulation of the notion of the free man in the limited state.

We have made a rapid survey of what Aristotelianism meant for the middle ages and the kind of philosophical activity which it provoked. This was the work of Christians, anxious to construct a synthesis of philosophy with the Christian faith, but determined that it should be a genuine philosophy built on reason and convinced that the progress of reason would both assist and illustrate their faith. While it would be altogether artificial to detach mediaeval philosophy from mediaeval theology, the philosophical systems of the middle ages are philosophies in the full sense of the word, and it would be equally mistaken either to accept their doctrines too hastily from sympathy with the corresponding theology or to reject them out of hand on account of dislike for it.

CHAPTER V

ST. BONAVENTURE

§ 1

THE three great mediaeval systems are those of Bonaventure, Aquinas and Duns Scotus. They are
all the result of the fruitful intermingling of the older
Augustinian tradition with the new Aristotelianism. Of
the three, Aquinas is the most Aristotelian and Bonaventure is the least, but it is impossible to represent
Bonaventure otherwise than as powerfully affected by
Aristotle. He was born in 1221, joined the Franciscan
order and studied at Paris under Alexander of Hales.
Later he became general of his order and a cardinal,
and died while taking part in the Council of Lyons in
1274. His philosophical doctrines are to be discovered
mainly in his commentary on the *Sentences* of Peter
Lombard; he also composed a number of *Quaestiones
Disputatae*, a summary of theology under the name of
the *Breviloquium,* and two shorter works of considerable
philosophical import, the *Itinerarium Mentis in Deum*
and the *De Reductione Artium ad Theologiam.*

While all the mediaeval systems are religious philosophies, that of Bonaventure is pre-eminently so. The
philosopher is most fully himself when he is not only
considering God in the comparatively external relationship to the world which consists in being its first cause
and last end but is seeking the traces of God in the
universe, the reflections of the divine being which is
the exemplar after which all things are framed. The

whole argument of the *Itinerarium Mentis in Deum* is the gradual unfolding of these intimations of deity in the created world.

Bonaventure found the mistakes of the pagan thinkers quite natural. He saw clearly and, with less care than Aquinas to save Aristotle's face, was prompt to declare that, according to Aristotle, the world was uncreated and eternal, and God had no thought or care for it. Although, absolutely speaking, right reason might have been sufficient to enlighten Aristotle on these questions, his errors were nevertheless only to be expected from a thinker without the support of faith. Yet, with the restoring power of faith and grace, Bonaventure attributed more to the human reason than Aquinas, for he expected it to be able to demonstrate that the world had a beginning, which Aquinas thought to be inaccessible to reason alone.

The general headings under which Bonaventure expounds his proofs of the existence of God are that this is a truth impressed upon all minds, a truth which every creature proclaims, and a truth which is in itself most certain and evident.[1] Under the first heading he insists that the natural human tendency towards the true and the good is implicitly a tendency towards the absolute truth and absolute good, which is God. The consciousness of the self naturally expands into an awareness of God, who is intimately present to the self. Hence the existence of God is not a question for subtle and complex argument; it becomes evident upon the least reflection.

These and similar utterances of Bonaventure have led

[1] Cf. *Qu. disp. de mysterio Trinitatis*, qu. i, art. i.

some critics to suppose that he was what in later terminology came to be called an ontologist, one who believed
that we naturally had some immediate knowledge of
God and a vision of all things in God. Grunwald, for
example, thinks that an other than ontologistic interpretation is scarcely possible.[1] This, however, seems to
be reading into Bonaventure a good deal more than is
really there. It is true that he describes his arguments
as rather intellectual exercises than reasons conferring
evidence upon the conclusion which they are intended
to prove. Yet, in the very next paragraph, he draws a
clear distinction between God's full comprehension of
himself, the immediate vision of God in heaven, and the
partial and relatively obscure knowledge of God which
men are capable of having on earth. This last is due to
the recognition of a supratemporal cause of man's
temporal existence, and is thus plainly the result of
reasoning, however brief and however obvious. It is
true, also, that Bonaventure speaks of the knowledge of
God as innate in the rational mind (*cognitio huius veri
innata est menti rationali*), but it would be an anti-
historical error to press this term in the sense of a later
philosophy which Bonaventure never anticipated. In
the context it appears clearly enough that Bonaventure
meant that the recognition of God was natural to man
and required only a momentary reflection and reasoning
to which nature itself impelled him. Philosophical arguments for the existence of God were merely the making
explicit and drawing out at length of a process of
thought which the natural man had already made spon-
taneously and implicitly.

[1] G. Grunwald: *Geschichte der Gottesbeweise im Mittelalter.* p. 130.

The arguments collected under the second and third headings are precisely the making explicit of the grounds upon which man naturally recognizes the existence of God. That every creature proclaims its creator, as Augustine had said, covers the different forms of the causal argument. Caused being proclaims uncaused being; possible being proclaims necessary being; limited being proclaims unlimited being; changeable being proclaims unchangeable being.

Under the heading that the existence of God is a truth certain and evident in itself, Bonaventure expounds both the ontological argument of Anselm and the Augustinian argument from eternal truth. He does not share St. Thomas's critical objections to the Anselmian argument, and is content to repeat it. On the whole, Bonaventure is not very critical of the various efforts made by his predecessors to make evident the truth of the existence of God, just because it is so very obvious to him. A more critical philosopher will perhaps discriminate the values of the different lines of thought set out by Bonaventure, but he will acknowledge in him the verification of the Pauline saying that God is not far from every one of us, at any rate if we think with rational impartiality and rational simplicity. It is not difficult to rise from contingent, caused and limited being to being which is necessary, uncaused and infinite, and this is God. Such, at least, is Bonaventure's position.

§ 2

On the burning question of the relationship between creation and time, Bonaventure stands firmly for the view that, as soon as the genuine notion of creation is established, it follows that the created world had a beginning. The great Arabic philosophers had thought differently. While the orthodox Mohammedan theologians held to the notion of creation as a beginning of time, and Alfarabi still regarded matter as emanating from God, Avicenna and Averroes set matter up as a principle coeternal with God and independent of him. With Avicenna this is a clear-cut dualism of a principle of utter being and a principle of utter non-being; with Averroes matter has more of being in so far as it actively tends towards form. For both, however, matter is eternal, and the mediate activity of God which confers form upon it and constitutes the cosmos is likewise eternal.

The Latin Averroists, as far as they dared, adopted the position of Averroes. Among the orthodox scholastics Albertus Magnus maintained that it could not be philosophically demonstrated that matter was created; this had to be accepted on grounds of religious faith. Given, however, that matter was created, it followed that the world could not have existed eternally. Aquinas took precisely the opposite view. That creation extended to all finite being and every principle of being, not excluding matter, was rationally demonstrable, but it could not be proved philosophically that the result of the creative act was not eternal, as was the creative act itself. It was the doctrine of a beginning of time which had to be accepted on faith.

Bonaventure here attributed greater power to reason than did either Albert or Thomas.[1] He shows himself

_____
[1] Cf. *In. II Sent.*, dist. 1, p. 1, art. I, qu. 2.

not uninfluenced by Albert, inasmuch as he appears to believe it to be more evident that, if matter was created, the world had a beginning, than that matter was indeed created. He remarks that, if matter were a principle uncreated and coeternal with God, it would be more reasonable to suppose that the divine action upon it was eternal than to think that this began at a moment separated from the present only by a finite duration. Nevertheless he maintains that it can be established that all being is from God and that, if this is so, it follows very clearly that the world had a beginning.

Some of his arguments are based on the difficulties connected with an infinite multitude. An infinite multitude, he says, cannot be increased, nor can it compose an ordered series of units which can be traversed one by one. But time is an ordered series which is traversed from moment to moment, and the number of moments is being continually increased. Moreover, if men had always existed, there would by now be an infinite multitude of souls, unless one were to take refuge in the erroneous hypothesis either of the transmigration of souls or of the unity of soul in the entire human race. But an infinite multitude of simultaneously existent things is surely an absurdity.

A critic might be disposed to judge that the modern mathematical theory of infinite numbers had taken the sting out of these arguments of Bonaventure. The series, say, of all whole numbers is an ordered infinite series. Nor are all infinite numbers equal or incapable of increase; the infinite number which is the sum of all even numbers can be added to the infinite number which is the sum of all odd numbers to make the infinite number which is the sum of all whole numbers. Bonaventure cannot, however, be refuted so easily. The success of a mathematical theory does not prove that the concepts with which it deals are not fictions but can be realized. Bonaventure might still retort that his arguments really concerned the application of the notion of infinite number to existent things. The point at issue is whether an infinite number is necessarily a fiction or not.

In any case there was another and more decisive consideration which prompted the opinion of Bonaventure. For he plainly believed that he discerned an essential connection between causality and time, such that being caused entailed having a beginning. He refers to Augustine's image of an eternal foot making an eternal footprint on an eternal ground. That is conceivable, he says in effect, but the ground would not in that case be created. If matter were eternal, God would not be the sole absolute being. Absolute being would comprise both God and matter; there might still be a relation of consequence between the divine activity and the information of matter, but this would not be what is meant by causation in the full sense of the term, and we could not speak of creation. He was evidently reaching out towards a distinction between a relation of real consequence which was indifferent to time and a relation of causation in which time was embodied, but the terminology was not available and he did not invent it. It is clear, however, that for Bonaventure, being created was inseparable from having a beginning, and his more discursive arguments were rather in the nature of confirmation of this primary acknowledgment.

§ 3

It was more or less common ground among the thinkers of the thirteenth century that the finiteness and changeability of things other than God was rooted in their being metaphysically composite. There was in them both a unity and a tension of opposed principles of being, related as determinable and determinant. Both with corporeal and with spiritual beings, Bonaventure speaks of this metaphysical composition in terms of matter and form. The modern reader must be warned that, in the mouth of Bonaventure, the statement that spirits are composed of matter and form does not imply that he held them to be material in the sense in which that word is now employed. For it is now usually taken as synonymous with corporeal, but for Bonaventure the "matter" of spiritual beings was very different from the matter of corporeal things.

This brings us to another point, that for Bonaventure the matter even of corporeal things is not the completely indeterminate principle of pure potentiality which is the first matter of Aristotle and the *materia prima* of St. Thomas Aquinas. The matter of sublunary bodies is already something in its own right, apart from form. In common with many other thinkers of the period, Bonaventure conceives corporeal matter in a way which belongs more to physics than to metaphysics. Matter is the ultimate substratum of bodies, and it is because all bodies have the same substratum that even the elementary bodies are capable of transformation one into another. Nevertheless, matter possesses a definite character as matter, for it is what all bodies have in common, and it possesses a seminal force to assume, under the appropriate conditions, the forms which it is capable of assuming.

In connection with the composition of things out of matter and form occurs the problem of the source of individuality. For matter, considered in abstraction, is the common element in all bodies. Form, on the other hand, is brought by the mediaeval thinkers into very close relation with the universal concept. To think in universal terms is to abstract form from matter. Forms, therefore, appear in abstraction to be universal elements, features which one thing shares, or may share, with others. With an analysis of things into matter and form, individuality seems to evaporate. Yet the individual alone is real. What is the metaphysical ground of individuality?

When Bonaventure considers this question, he remarks that some attribute individuation to matter on the ground that forms are the objects of universal concepts, while matter makes them real and, consequently, individual. Others, however, regarding individuality as the final perfection of the existent thing, attribute it to a final form supervening upon merely specific determination. Bonaventure comments bluntly that it does not require much intelligence to see that neither view is satisfactory (*Quaelibet istarum positionum aliquid habet, quod homini non multum intelligenti rationabiliter videri poterit improbabile*). For matter is common to all bodies, while form must be upheld to be correlative with the universal concept.

Bonaventure's own opinion is that individuality arises from the actual conjunction of matter with form. He

compares matter with wax and form with a seal; the
wax is not differentiated until it is impressed with the
seal, while the seal remains one in itself and only its
impressions are multiplied. In the sequel, however, he
comes nearer to the view which we shall find to be that
of Aquinas. To be an individual, he says, is to be *hoc
aliquid,* this thing of a determinate nature. But to be
this results primarily from matter, on account of which
a thing is situated in space and time, while its determinate nature is the contribution of form. Hence matter
confers existence upon form, and form makes matter to
be something determinate (*Existere dat materia formae,
sed essendi actum dat forma materiae*).[1]

§ 4

For the human soul, as having an activity of thought
and will which is independent of the body, Bonaventure
vindicates a considerable degree of substantial independence. While the body is composed of corporeal matter
and corporeal form, the soul is composed of spiritual
matter and spiritual form. Bonaventure mentions the
opinion of those who, like Aquinas, assigned to the soul
no other composition than that of essence and existence,
but he objects that this is insufficient to make it a subject
of independent change and activity. Where there is
change, he maintains, there must be a principle of
plasticity and tendency, and this is precisely matter in
its widest meaning.

This applies only to the human soul; the vital principle of brute animals, which has no activity independent

[1] Cf. *In. II Sent.,* dist. 3, p. 1, art. 2, qu. 3.

of the organism, must be regarded as no more than a
corporeal form. The human soul, although composed of
matter and form, is not spatially extended. Bonaventure
repels this notion by insisting once again on the distinction between corporeal matter, which entails spatial
extension, and spiritual matter, which is a principle of
plasticity exempt from spatial limitations.

Nor will he admit that his theory makes body and
soul into separate substances. Matter and form make
up a complete substance when their union exhausts their
mutual tendencies, but, in the case of human nature, the
soul has a further tendency or appetite towards an
appropriate organism, and the human body has a similar
appetite to be completed by the soul. Hence, while the
soul can and, after death, does exist and act separately,
it is still not substantially complete in itself; body and
soul are both necessary to full human nature. This, it
must be confessed, sounds more like an ingenious verbal
expedient than a really satisfactory answer.[1]

Bonaventure names the faculties of the soul in
Augustinian fashion as memory, understanding and will.
On the question of the relationship between the soul
and its faculties he does not profess to have attained
complete clearness, but he makes an interesting attempt
to reach a satisfactory point of view. It has always been
a difficult matter to define. If powers are put on a level
with actual qualities, they cease to be powers and begin
to masquerade as explanatory factors, like the *virtus
dormitiva* of which Molière made fun. But it is evident
that they belong to the sphere of description and not of
explanation. They are not, however, mere names; to

[1] Cf. *In. II Sent.*, dist. 17, art. 1, qu. 2.

say that a man has the power of thinking is really significant, even when he is not actually thinking. Bonaventure rejects both extremes. He rejects the opinion which reduces a power to a mere relation between the substance and its activity, in spite of the ostensible authority of Augustine. This would make a power to be nothing at all when the substance is in fact inactive. He rejects also the opinion, attributed to Hugh of St. Victor, that powers are qualities like other qualities and mutually distinguished in the way in which accidental qualities are distinguished. The formula at which he arrives states that powers are not accidental determinations of substance but belong reductively to the sphere of substance itself; nevertheless they are not to be completely identified with substance, for they differ from it and among themselves precisely as powers.[1]

§ 5

Bonaventure's view of the nature of thinking is a characteristic part of his philosophy. He is the most prominent exponent of a theory of divine illumination of the intellect which had many supporters among the more Augustinian scholastics. Its ancestry is plainly to be found in the Platonic system of ideas which are at the same time ideals, standards which are only imperfectly realized in the objects of experience but in relation to which these objects are judged by the mind. Justice is but poorly manifested in human affairs, but we judge the actions of men by a consummate standard of justice which is justice itself. No individual man realizes all of

[1] Cf. In. II Sent., dist. 24, p. 1, art. 2, qu. 1.

which h man nature is capable, but we judge the worth of men in accordance with a standard of perfect humanity. Augustine indicated this feature of thinking as the point of contact between the human mind and the eternal truth of God, and as a means by which it could be seen that there existed an eternal truth which was no other than the mind of God. Many of the scholastics, and among them Bonaventure, drew this out into a theory of the divine illumination of the human mind in its natural activity.

It is made quite clear by Bonaventure that this illumination signifies more than the universal creative causation by which God is the source of all things. If it were only this, he says, God could not be said to bestow wisdom in any fuller sense than he makes the earth fruitful, nor could knowledge be held to proceed more directly from him than wealth.[1] On the other hand, it is altogether different from the vision of God which is the privilege of heaven and proceeds not from nature but from grace. If not, then, from God simply as *principium creativum*, and not from him as *donum infusum*, this illumination must be said to be from him as *ratio movens*.

It must be confessed that Bonaventure's positive view is lacking in final precision. It would be tempting to father some clearcut interpretation upon him, but it would be unhistorical and probably unjust. Perhaps a useful clue is afforded by his use of the word *imago*. A created thing, he says, is related to the divine exemplar as trace, image or likeness (*vestigium, imago, similitudo*). Material things are merely *vestigia Dei;* likeness

---

[1] *Qu. disp. de Scientia Christi*, qu. 4.

in the full sense (*similitudo*) belongs only to the supernatural life; but a created mind is already by its nature *imago Dei*. In what way can human thinking be said to be in a special sense an image of the divine mind? Bonaventure would point to ideal standards and to the necessity and certainty of genuine universal propositions as possessing a character which transcends the contingent particular things to which they may be applied. There is a sense in which we may be said to judge contingent things with reference to a truth which is superior to them, which is in fact absolute. It is not that we have a direct vision of absolute truth, but absolute truth is implied in the higher functions of the understanding. In the universality and necessity of thinking we reflect in a special way the activity of the divine mind. The created mind is *imago Dei*.

In the third chapter of the *Itinerarium Mentis in Deum* Bonaventure applies this conception to the whole mental life. Memory, taken in Augustinian fashion as the primary function of mind in static simplicity, reflects the divine mind in more than one way. In envisaging past, present and future it transcends the successiveness of time and reflects the divine eternity. In the formation of pure abstractions such as points and moments it displays a power independent of and superior to the influence of the objects of sense. In the apprehension of immutable general truths it reflects the unchangingness of God.

Similar considerations are alleged about the understanding as the discursive function of mind. The penetration of the meaning of a term, which is to define it, is incomplete until it is resolved into the notion of being, and until what kind of being the thing is can be stated. But the limitation of a finite being cannot be understood without some sort of knowledge of the positive perfection of which it is devoid. Hence a genuine comprehension of the nature of anything is at the same time an implicit recognition of infinite being too. So also the certainty of general truths and the necessity of inferences cannot be derived exclusively from the contingent and changing facts which provide their material.

Of the will Bonaventure says that deliberation about what is better implies some conception of what is best, that right choice depends upon the recognition of a law superior to finite mind, and that desire of any good presupposes the universal attraction of absolute good. "See, therefore, how near the soul is to God, and how memory presents it with eternity, understanding with truth, and choice with absolute goodness, each by its proper activity."

These instances of Bonaventure are not beyond cavil, and a critical analysis might reduce their claims and make them yield more modest, although more precise, conclusions. Our present business, however, is rather to describe than to appraise. Yet, even if Bonaventure is not so exact a thinker as he might be, and even if he sometimes mistakes for a premiss leading to the acknowledgment of the divine being what is really a conclusion from it, we should not fail to perceive the core of hard thinking which gives solidity to his work. His absorption in God is that not only of a religious man but of a genuine metaphysician.

CHAPTER VI

ST. THOMAS AQUINAS

§ 1

THE greatest of mediaeval thinkers came from an Italian family of Norman descent. The son of a count of Aquino, he was born at Roccasecca in 1225. In spite of the opposition of his family he entered the Dominican order in 1244, and his life thereafter is a record of study, teaching and writing. He died in 1274 at Fossanuova on his way to the Council of Lyons.

Into this comparatively short lifetime St. Thomas crowded an immense literary output. His best known works are the two great syntheses of the *Summa Theologica* and the *Summa contra Gentes*. A complete understanding of his philosophy requires also the study of his opuscula, such as *De Ente et Essentia, De Aeternitate Mundi* and *De Unitate Intellectus,* his *quaestiones disputatae,* especially *De Veritate,* and his commentaries on Aristotle, especially those on the *Metaphysics* and *De Anima.*

While wholeheartedly Aristotelian in his principles, he made full use also of the older Augustinian and Neoplatonic tradition. The result, however, is not simply a blend of Augustine and Aristotle; it is Thomism. Aquinas did what any powerful thinker should aim at doing, neither slavishly following his predecessors nor constructing a new system in utter disregard of what had been thought by others, but bringing an original mind to the work of rethinking and completing the results of previous inquiry.

In one way the best tribute to his originality was the opposition which he provoked from more conservative minds. Three years after his death, Stephen Tempier, bishop of Paris, in condemning the opinions of the Averroists, attacked also some of the Thomistic theses. At the same period two archbishops of Canterbury, Robert Kilwardby, himself a Dominican, and the Franciscan John Peckham, spoke out forcibly against Thomism. William de la Mare produced a *Correctorium fratris Thomae,* which was answered by the *Correctorium corruptorii fratris Thomae.* The Dominicans, however, were gradually won over to Aquinas, and attacks on his orthodoxy naturally ceased from any quarter after his canonization in 1323. He became acknowledged as the greatest doctor of the middle ages, and in modern times the Church has once again strongly recommended not only his theology but also his philosophy. The justification of this is to be found in the truth that he was in fact the most eminent thinker of a period which gave its deepest attention to the philosophical questions which border on theology and provide the foundation of a religious view of the world. A fruitful Thomism must, of course, set out to rethink and add to his work as he set out to rethink and add to the work of his predecessors.

§ 2

The mediaeval thinkers did not develop a theory of knowledge in the sense in which it is understood nowadays; they took common sense for granted and did not inquire systematically into the meaning and validity of our spontaneous convictions. Aquinas is no exception to this rule, but he has a theory of knowledge in another sense; he has a clearly defined conception of what knowledge is and what in particular is the range of human knowledge.

Knowledge and being are correlative. In so far as a thing is, it is knowable, and in this resides its ontological truth. Hence, whatever the difficulties inherent in specific fields of knowledge, Aquinas would have dismissed as a pseudo-problem the question whether we are capable of genuine knowledge of anything at all or are rather, according to the idealistic contention, condemned to a perpetual spinning out of ourselves of ideas whose correspondence with fact remains doubtful. Thomism maintains a wholehearted epistemological realism.

But, while the object of the intellect in general is being in general, the specific object of the human intellect is the being of sensible things. St. Thomas is completely Aristotelian in finding the whole material of thought in sense-experience. Thomism is, therefore, a philosophy of experience, but it is not a mere empiricism, which stops short at sense-experience and refuses to see in the development of thought anything but an elaboration of sensations and images. Aquinas himself presents the Aristotelian view as a mean between two extremes.[1] The one is the theory of Democritus which reduces all knowledge to sensation and imagination; the other is the Platonic outlook, according to which sensa-

[1] Cf. *Summa Theologica* I, qu. 84, art. vi.

tion provides no more than the occasion upon which the understanding comes to contemplate the spiritual world of forms. Aristotle, he says, finds the happy mean by recognizing that all knowledge is derived from sense-experience, but at the same time asserting that thought has its proper activity, by which it can draw from sense-experience the materials of a knowledge which extends beyond the bounds of the world of sense.

Thinking penetrates through the particular to the universal. Particulars are in fact instances of universals, but it is not until thinking has done its work that universals as such are brought before the mind. In sense-experience we are acquainted with red things; by thinking we come to isolate the redness which these things manifest. At the same time we come to see an order in the attributes manifested by the objects of experience; we come to see what they essentially are as distinguished from what they happen to be. In other words, thinking penetrates to the substance of things and distinguishes this from the accidents. The Abelardian theory of abstraction serves St. Thomas as a beginning, but *intelligere* is also *intus legere*. Thinking arrives at the essences of things.

The intellect, then, is both active and passive. As passive it receives its material from sense-experience; as active it elaborates this by abstraction and by its consequent penetration through the unanalysed superficiality of sensation. Hence, with Aristotle, we must make a distinction between *intellectus possibilis* and *intellectus agens*. But St. Thomas is quite certain that the nature of anything suffices for the performance of its natural operations; he will have none of the theories, whether

Arab or Latin, which make the *intellectus agens* something distinct from the individual mind. The active intellect is a part of the soul, and consequently each human soul possesses its own active intellect.[1] This we know not only on grounds of general principle but also from experience; we are conscious of our own activity of thought when we bring our mental powers to bear upon the material provided by sensation. Hence, while Aquinas was willing to adopt the formula of a divine illumination of the mind, this took on for him a new meaning which excluded the necessity of a special divine assistance at every moment of the activity of thought. The intellect is by its nature a participation of the divine light and, once created, it has in itself all that is needed for the fulfilment of the purpose for which it is naturally intended.[2]

The mind, aware that its concepts are derived from fact and are attributable to fact, is conscious of possessing truth and of being by its nature orientated towards truth. In the building up of knowledge it has at its disposal two kinds of truths. It makes judgments about the particular facts which enter into its experience, and it makes judgments about the relations of its concepts in the abstract. Primitive judgments of the latter kind are *principia per se nota,* general propositions which contain their evidence in themselves. The generative process by which the sciences are constructed is now apparent; general principles are applied to the facts of common-sense experience, and a series of deductions is the result.

---

[1] Cf. *S. Th.* I, qu. 79, art. iv-v, and *De Unitate Intellectus contra Averroistas.*
[2] Cf. *S. Th.* I, qu. 84, art. v.

St. Thomas was not unaware that many theories, especially about the material world, do not enter into this scheme of simple deductive inference. He acknowledged that the Ptolemaic astronomy current at his time could not be deduced from the facts of observation. While accepting it as an hypothesis which fitted the facts, he admitted that some other system might fit the facts equally well or better.[1] Such remarks show that he could have appreciated the methods by which the physical sciences have developed in modern times, but his real interest was in the genuinely philosophical questions to which a deductive method is appropriate.

§ 3

The Thomistic conception of matter and form is entirely metaphysical, and consequently independent of changes in the sciences of observation. All corporeal substances, and corporeal substances only, are composed of matter and form. First matter (*materia prima*) is a principle of pure potentiality in the order of essence. Since it is pure potentiality, it cannot exist by itself, for to exist is to be actually something, and matter becomes actually something only by receiving form.

The principle of pure potentiality which is *materia prima* is the source of the difference between corporeal and spiritual beings. Cognition springs from the possession of form without matter. Hence, when the form is completely immersed in matter, we have a purely corporeal being without cognition, in so far as the form has a certain independence of matter, there arise the

[1] Cf. *S. Th.* I, qu. 32, art. i, ad. 2 m.

various stages of cognitive experience. It should be noted that Aquinas is far from the utter dichotomy of mind and matter which we find in Descartes and which we are nowadays inclined to assume without reflection. There are degrees of immateriality. The experiences of a purely sentient being, an animal, have already a certain immateriality; human mind, enjoying a greater degree of immateriality, is capable of an activity of thought which is intrinsically independent of the organism; and beyond human thinking there are purely spiritual beings, subsistent forms without matter, the angels, whose activity is one of pure thought.

The metaphysical analysis of a corporeal thing, therefore, is into first matter and substantial form, this whole substance being matter in another sense for the reception of accidental forms, some of which, its essential powers and qualities are necessarily consequent upon the substance of the thing, while others vary from time to time according to circumstances. One of the typical theses of St. Thomas, although it was not completely without precedent, is that one substance has only one substantial form. It was this opinion which was stigmatized by Kilwardby as *fatua positio*. Most of the other scholastics regarded an organism as containing a hierarchy of substantial forms, but Aquinas maintains a solidarity between substantial form and substantial existence. The first form bestows substantial existence, and any additional form can only be accidental. If an organism had a plurality of substantial forms, it would not be one substance but many. After some initial hesitations in his early *Commentary on the Sentences,* this became the mature view of St. Thomas, and he asserts it as a disputed point with great vigour and determination in his later works.

The principle of individuation of corporeal things is *materia quantatate signata*. The form, considered in conceptual abstraction, is common to all members of the species. It is *this* form only because it is received by *this* matter, for matter, although it is in itself entirely indeterminate, is *this* matter in the sense that it is the source of quantitative extension, and the matter of each thing demands a certain determinate extension. The beginner may obtain a vague approximation to the Thomistic view by thinking of the multiplication of individuals within a species as due to the species having instances in different parts of space and time, but he should remember that the metaphysical analysis of St. Thomas is concerned with the principles of substance itself, which are logically prior to actual positions in space and time. Hence a purely spiritual being, which does not occupy space, can be said to be at the same time an individual and a species.

§ 4

Since man as a whole, though blended of the corporeal and the spiritual, is one substance, body and soul cannot be rightly thought of as two complete entities. The soul, in Aristotelian phrase, is the form of the body (*anima est forma corporis*). It is the soul which, by informing matter, is the principle of bodily structure and organic life, of sensation and of thought. If anyone, says St. Thomas, wanted to say that the thinking mind is not the substantial form of the human organism, he would have to discover how in that case thinking could be attributed to a man as his own activity. For we are conscious that it is we who think, just as we know that it is we who are corporeal beings. If soul and body were united merely by their constant interaction, there would be two selves instead of one, a mental self and a bodily self. Similarly, if it were held, with Bonaventure, that soul and body were each composed of matter and form, we should be left with two selves again. The only formula which does justice to the substantial unity of human nature is the Aristotelian proposition that the soul is the form of the body.[1]

But, Aquinas adds, there is a gradation in the way in which forms dominate matter. The less a form is immersed in matter, the greater the activity which it manifests. The human soul is a form which transcends matter to such an extent that it possesses in thinking an activity of its own, intrinsically independent of matter. Upon this foundation rests the truth of personal immortality. For whatever has an activity of its own is capable of independent existence; hence the corruption of the body, while putting an end to organic and sentient activity, does not involve the destruction of the thinking mind.[2] The same complete immateriality of thought is the reason why the origin of each individual human soul cannot be attributed simply to the forces of matter but is the result of a special creative activity of God.[3] This does not mean that every human soul is of miraculous origin. It comes to be in accordance with the laws of nature and whenever the appropriate material condi-

[1] Cf. S. Th. I, qu. 76, art. i.
[2] Cf. S. Th. I, qu. 75, art. ii and vi.
[3] Cf. S. Th. I, qu. 118, art. ii.

tions are present, but the relation of the divine causality to its origin is of a special kind and different from the general concurrence which God, in consequence of his creative will, gives to purely material processes.

The possession of the power of abstract and analytic thought entails the freedom of the will. All natural tendency is towards the good or value appropriate to the subject of tendency. The desire of a sentient subject goes automatically and instinctively towards the concrete value which it apprehends. A thinking mind, however, is able to conceive good in general and, therefore, to reach out towards a fullness of good in relation to which all finite values are deficient. Confronted with any finite value, it can appreciate both its positive value and its deficiency. Hence no finite value is by itself sufficient to determine rational choice.[1]

There remain the general problem of the source of rational choice and the particular problem of the relation to rational choice of the universal divine causality. St. Thomas is clear that while the acts of the human will are genuinely free, they are yet not exempt from divine causation, but he says that the divine activity is proportioned to its objects, so that necessary causes produce their effects of necessity and contingent causes in a contingent manner. It is the very efficacy of the divine causation which ensures that those things which God wills do not only come into being but come into being in the way in which he wills them and in which they correspond with the natures of the agents through which he brings them about.[2]

[1] Cf. *S. Th.* I, qu. 82, art. i and ii, qu. 83, art. i.
[2] Cf. *S. Th.* I, qu. 19, art. viii.

Evidently a difference of emphasis is possible in the interpretation of these statements. Either the emphasis is placed on the efficacy of the divine causation, and we are left with the paradox that God determines a free agent to make this particular choice, but to make it freely; or the emphasis is placed on the freedom of rational will, and it becomes difficult to see what the divine causation precisely determines. Hence the rise of two opposed schools of thought on the subject in later scholasticism is quite intelligible. But, we say, surely Aquinas must have seen the difficulty. Presumably he did see it, and presumably also he never arrived at an answer which satisfied himself, or he would have expressed himself more definitely. He presents us with the two factors which would have to be taken into account for any adequate solution, but their final reconciliation remains obscure. That he could not dissipate this obscurity need not be shocking.

§ 5

The metaphysics of St. Thomas centre in his analysis of existence. We have already noticed that he rejected the ontological argument, by which St. Anselm sought to infer the existence from the nature of God. It seems fair to suspect that the invalidity of this argument is due to some special characteristic of the notion of existence. Aquinas, in fact, for the first time in the history of philosophy, indicates the course of reflection by which we may come to appreciate the uniqueness of existence.

Since being is the most universal of all notions, it might seem that it was a supreme genus of which all kinds of being are the species and all individual beings the members. Yet, following Aristotle, St. Thomas points out that being is not a genus.[1] A properly generic notion is, as a notion, complete in itself, and the factors which serve as its specific differences are completely outside it. The notion of an animal is completely defined as a sentient organism, and the possession of reason, which differentiates human animality, is conceptually altogether separate from it. But the different kinds of being are beings as much in that in which they differ as in that in which they agree; every mode of being is itself an existent somewhat. If you try to separate being from anything or from any factor in anything, this becomes nothing; everything, and every factor in everything, is something.

It follows that being is not a true generic notion which can be conceptually cut off from the factors which differentiate it. A genuine universal concept is a principle of identity in those particulars which verify it. All animals, in so far as they are animals or sentient organisms, are alike. It is true that all animals verify animality together with a difference which, in reality, is inseparable from it, but, to abstract thinking, animality represents a complete and self-contained concept. While a genuine universal concept is an identity which connotes a difference, it is in itself a unity for thought. The notion of being, on the other hand, is at the same time a principle of identity and a principle of difference; it permeates its own modes. Being is in itself an identity in difference, while a genuine universal concept is merely an identity which connotes a difference.

[1] Cf. *Summa contra Gentiles* I, 25.

That is why there is so close a connection between the notion of being and that of individuality. An excessive realism in the solution of the problem of universals falls before the Aristotelian principle that the individual alone exists in the proper sense of the term. We may now go farther and say that what in the individual corresponds with the universals which it verifies is not the intrinsic ground of its individuality; it is because it is an existent, and precisely through its substantial existence or subsistence, that it is this individual thing. While the principle of individuation of corporeal species is matter, the general principle of individuality is substantial existence or subsistence.

In this way we are led to distinguish between the order of essence and the order of existence. The order of essence represents in abstraction the ramification and interrelation of universal concepts; the order of existence runs parallel with it and lends to it individuality and reality. Existence, therefore, is proportional to essence, to that which exists. Existence is not a closed generic concept which is specified by the differences of essences; it is in itself different, and must be regarded as greater or less, according to the nature of that which it makes to exist. Here lies the fundamental significance of the analogy of being. Analogy, after all, means proportion, and the analogy of being means that the existence of each thing is proportionate to its essence.

If essence and existence are thus proportionate, there is in every finite thing between its essence and its existence a certain metaphysical tension, which in scholastic language is described as metaphysical composition. While existence realizes essence, essence provides the limits within which existence is circumscribed. There is in the application to essence and existence of the Aristotelian concepts of potentiality and actuality a shade of ambiguity which may have contributed to later doubts and controversies on the subject. For, although existence determines essence in the sense of realizing it, essence determines existence in the sense of specifying it. In order, therefore, to appreciate the Thomistic theory of essence and existence, it is necessary to look at these notions for their own sake without expecting to fit them exactly into some preconceived general formula. The notion of existence is unique, and St. Thomas helps us powerfully to understand its uniqueness. In so doing he opens the way to his philosophical conception of God.

§ 6

Aquinas makes plain that, since the primary object of the human intellect is the being of sensible things, we have naturally no direct knowledge of God, nor is there any short cut to his existence by a purely conceptual argument such as that of Anselm. The existence of God must be the object of a demonstration whose force depends in part upon the existence of the things of experience. The foundations of this demonstration are laid in the Five Ways.[1]

The first three ways are variant forms of what in modern times is usually called the cosmological argument. The First Way is described in the *Summa Theologica* as especially obvious (*manifestior*). This epithet should probably be interpreted in the light of the much

[1] The Five Ways in *S. Th.* I, qu. 2, art. iii. Cf. *S. c. G.* I, 13.

lengthier formulation of the proof in the *Summa contra Gentiles,* where Aquinas employs all the resources of Aristotelian physics to conclude, as Aristotle had done, to the existence of the first unmoved mover. Such a proof would, for the mediaeval man, have conjured up a mental picture in terms of contemporary astronomy, and in this way would have been for him *manifestior.* For us now, and reduced to its metaphysical essentials as it is in the *Summa Theologica,* it could hardly be said to be more obvious than the Second or Third Way. It is an argument from *motus,* which serves as a Latin rendering for κίνησις and, like κίνησις, has a wide range of meaning from locomotion in particular through continuous change to change in general. For the essential metaphysical purpose of St. Thomas's argument, as distinguished from the mental picture which he hoped to summon up in order to make it more obvious, *motus* is best understood as change in general. Any change, then, presupposes an agency which brings it about, and, if the agent is itself subject to change, this can only be under the influence of another agent. Such a series of agencies cannot be infinite. The supposition that every agent is moved by a higher agent is self-contradictory, for there would then be no ground for the process as a whole. Hence there must be a first unmoved mover, an agent which is not itself subject to change but is the primary source of the series of changes which we observe to take place.

The First Way envisages change from the point of view of the effect which requires an agent; the Second Way proceeds directly from the fact of causation. We observe instances of the relation of cause and effect, and we find that the cause is itself the effect of another cause. This series cannot be infinite, for, if nothing could cause without being caused, there would be nothing to set the causal series going. Hence we must conclude to the existence of an uncaused cause.

The Third Way shifts the point of view yet a little again and proceeds from the notions of necessity and contingency. From the fact that things come into being and cease to be, we see that they are not necessary but contingent or capable of non-existence. Here Aquinas reproduces the suggestion of Maimonides that, if everything were capable of non-existence, there would actually be a time at which nothing existed, and in that case nothing could ever come to exist. Whatever may be thought of this, it is clear that the ultimate source of the coming-to-be of the contingent must be sought in the necessarily existent. Aquinas then takes into account Avicenna's hypothetical distinction between a being which is necessary but derivative and a being which is necessary of itself; the former would be something which necessarily and eternally emanates from the source of all being. Even if there were such derivatively necessary existents, there must be in the end something which is necessary of itself and from which they would derive their necessity.

By the first three ways, therefore, St. Thomas has arrived at the existence of unchanging, uncaused and intrinsically necessary being. He has not yet discussed what sort of being this must be, but, by an anticipation of the later course of his argument, he says that this is to be identified with God. It is worth remarking that his proofs do not depend upon the supposition that the world has had a finite duration; in fact we shall see that he does not regard this as philosophically demonstrable. According to Aquinas it is philosophically conceivable that there should have been an infinite series of caused events succeeding one another, but it is not philosophically conceivable that a series of caused causes, whether finite or infinite, should not ultimately depend upon an uncaused cause outside the series.

The Fourth and Fifth Ways appear as supplementary to this main argument. The Fifth Way is the familiar teleological argument which concludes to an intelligence governing the world, but St. Thomas is content to enucleate it very briefly. The Fourth Way has aroused more discussion. It proceeds from the degrees of being which are observable in the world about us to the existence of an absolute and supreme being. In form it is historically most nearly akin to the kind of proof which St. Anselm uses in the *Monologion,* and the texts of Aristotle to which St. Thomas appeals are in reality from the pseudo-Aristotelian book, *Metaphysics a.* Where you observe, he says, things which are more or less somewhat, you must suppose something which is absolutely and completely so. Where, then, you observe degrees of being, you must conclude that an absolute and supreme being exists. Grunwald is so scandalized that he remarks *dass wir es hier mit einem rein abstrakt begrifflichen Beweisverfahren zu tun haben, das in idealistischer Art aus blossen Begriffen auf die Wirklichkeit schliesst, und zwar mit einer überraschenden Offenheit und Schroffheit, wie wir sie nur in der Frühscholastik antrafen.*[1] The truth seems to be that Grunwald has

[1] G. Grunwald: *Geschichte der Gottesbeweise im Mittelalter,* p. 155.

been so overwhelmed by the admittedly rather summary terms in which Aquinas expresses himself that he fails to notice that the Fourth Way really amounts to an anticipation of the line of thought by which the being whose existence is demonstrated by the first three ways is seen to be identical with what we usually mean by God. To this we now turn.

St. Thomas has, then, proved the existence of unchanging, uncaused, necessary being. When he goes on to explore what sort of being this must be, it is the notion of being itself which supplies the most characteristically Thomistic line of argument. Contingent things participate in existence, each according to the degree which corresponds with its nature or essence, but they are not their own existence. If their essence included their existence, they would not be contingent but necessary. The privilege of necessary being is that in reality its essence includes or is really identical with its existence.[1]

In a necessary being, therefore, there is no composition or metaphysical tension of essence and existence. Essence does not limit or circumscribe existence; necessary being is being itself and pure act (*ipsum esse, actus purus*). If, then, we want to know what we can say about it, we must begin with the notion of being and see that it must comprise all that being positively can be. "Since God is subsistent being itself, nothing of the perfection of being can be wanting in him. The perfections of all things are contained in the perfection of being, for things are perfect in so far as they possess a degree of being; whence it follows that God does not lack the

[1] Cf. *S. Th.* I, qu. 3, art. iii-iv.

perfection of anything."[1] The ontological argument was invalid, because it proceeded from the mere notion of infinite being to its actual and necessary existence; St. Thomas, on the other hand, has proved by the application of a causal principle to the facts of experience that a necessary being exists, and can now argue validly that a necessary being must, as pure being, be infinite. Since there can be only one infinite being, there can be only one God, and, since all pure perfections are contained in God, God must be the supreme intelligence and will. God, therefore, is supremely personal, and this is the real God of religion who revealed himself to Moses as *I am who am* and revealed himself fully and finally in the Incarnate Word. The perfection of the infinite being must inconceivably transcend our finite conceptions, but we have a genuine philosophical knowledge of God as far as it goes. We know that he is infinite being, and that we can rightly attribute to him in its supreme degree and without any admixture of limitation all that we find of perfection in the created world. As we have an analogical knowledge of being, so we have an analogical knowledge of God. With this insight St. Thomas corrects the relatively agnostic attitude of Maimonides, who tends to reduce us to mere negations when we come to speak of God.

God, as subsistent being, is the source of all that in a finite manner participates being. Hence it is a philosophical truth that God is the creator of all things and of every factor in reality, even of *materia prima*.[2]

---

[1] *S. Th.* I, qu. 4, art. ii. For this whole development cf. esp. E. Gilson: *God and Philosophy*, pp. 62-73.
[2] Cf. *S. Th.* I, qu. 44, art. i-ii.

Aquinas recognizes that Aristotle held the world to have existed eternally, but denies that the reasons given for this opinion are conclusive. The existence of the world is the result of the divine fiat, but it is not necessary that created things should share in the eternity of the creative will. On the contrary, the power of the divine will is such that things exist after the fashion, and specifically with the temporal character, assigned to them by the will of God. It is not, therefore, absurd to assert that the created world had a beginning.

Nevertheless, according to St. Thomas, this cannot be philosophically demonstrated. Since universal concepts are independent of time, they can be instantiated at any time and might be instantiated eternally. Creation belongs to the sphere of divine freedom of choice, which cannot be explored by us on general grounds. Hence there can be no demonstrative reason, either on the part of God or on the part of creatures, by which we could conclude that the world had a beginning. While this is a truth of divine revelation, it cannot be brought into the ambit of philosophy, and St. Thomas issues a friendly warning against trying to provide strictly revealed truths with inadequate philosophical proofs *quae praebeant materiam irridendi infidelibus.*[1]

§ 7

St. Thomas's moral philosophy is a masterly theistic adaptation of the scheme of the *Nicomachean Ethics* of Aristotle. Aristotelian eudaemonism might not seem at first sight a very suitable foundation for a theistic ethic.

[1] Cf. *S. Th.* I, qu. 46, art. i-ii, and *De Aeternitate Mundi.*

The notion of obligation takes a subordinate place in Aristotle's theory, although it is not completely absent, for it appears in the form that the good man acts for the sake of the noble (τοῦ καλοῦ ἕνεκα). But the main object of Aristotle's inquiry is, on the assumption that the sense of human striving can be summed up in the complete and lasting happiness which is εὐδαιμονία, to ask in what this happiness consists. The answer is given entirely in factors intrinsic to human nature. Happiness consists in the harmonious development and co-ordination of natural human activities, and especially in the intellectual life, which is the development of the highest part of man and promises a contentment which is uniquely durable and independent of circumstances. This seems to be an eminently self-contained human ethic, in fact *une morale laïque.*

There is a dramatic element in watching how, in the *Prima Secundae,* this is quietly but adroitly transformed into a theistic ethic. The last end of man is described as beatitude, which serves to render εὐδαιμονία, and Aquinas placidly demonstrates that beatitude cannot arise from external or bodily goods. When, however, he has thus narrowed his search to the region of spirit, he does not, like Aristotle, rest in the praises of the intellectual life. While it must be through the soul that man attains to beatitude, he says that the good of which the possession is the source of beatitude must be something beyond the soul itself. For, being aware by thought of good in general, we cannot but hanker after the completeness of good, but any good which is entirely within the soul must be a particular and finite good. Beatitude, therefore, can consist in nothing less than the possession of the supreme good which is God himself. The final aim of man is no longer an immanent perfection but a union with the transcendent Deity.[1]

In what does this possession of God consist? St. Thomas says that it must be primarily an intellectual activity. It is clearly not a desire, for this precedes the attainment of good; nor is it primarily joy, for this is a consequence of the fulfilment of desire rather than the fulfilment itself. Beatitude, then, consists essentially in intellectual activity, and obviously in the speculative state of contemplation rather than in the practical use of mind which is reaching out towards goods to be attained. While St. Thomas asserts from experience that speculative knowledge such as we can have in this life is a foretaste of true and perfect beatitude, he realizes that such knowledge is too scrappy and incomplete to be beatitude itself. Beatitude is not knowledge about God but acquaintance with God, the vision of the divine essence.[2]

In this way St. Thomas's ethic has linked up with his theology, and in so doing has raised a problem. For the vision of God is not natural to man and cannot be attained by his natural activity, yet it seems that he cannot fulfil himself completely and reach beatitude without it. Although the Christian finds the solution of the difficulty in the supernatural life of grace, this is a free gift of God, and the philosopher as such is not entitled to assume that God wills to bestow it. Aquinas puts the objection to himself that "nature is not lacking in what is necessary. But nothing is so necessary to

[1] Cf. *S. Th.* Ia. IIae, qu. 2.
[2] Cf. *S. Th.* Ia. IIae, qu. 3.

man as that through which he reaches his last end. Therefore this is not lacking to human nature. Hence man can by his natural powers reach beatitude". He replies that, "as nature is not lacking in what is necessary to man, although it did not provide him with weapons and coverings like the animals, because it provided him with reason and hands by which he could obtain these for himself, so it is not lacking in what is necessary to man, although it did not provide him with the power to reach beatitude, for this was impossible; but it provided him with free will, by which he could turn to God who would confer beatitude upon him".[1] The point is sound, but questioning is not altogether stilled. In fact this problem of a natural tendency towards a supernatural end remains a centre of discussion in the Thomistic system.

The Thomistic approach to ethics is, therefore, thoroughly teleological and heteronomous, and appears in extreme contrast with an approach of the Kantian kind through the notion of pure obligation. Obligation arises in the choice of the means which are genuinely appropriate towards the end of beatitude, but the egoistic element is transcended in the specific character of obligations which are not self-regarding. If moral striving is directed not simply towards beatitude, but towards God who is the source of beatitude, it follows that right action must be in conformity with the divine will, which is directed towards the common good of the universe as the created participation of the divine goodness itself. "Hence, in order that anyone should rightly will any particular good, it is necessary that,

[1] S. Th. Ia. IIae, qu. 5, art. v, 1 et ad 1m.

although what is materially willed is this particular good, what is formally willed should be the common good and the divine good. Therefore the human will is bound to conform with the divine will in its formal object, for it is bound to will the common and divine good."[1]

In relation to human nature an action is right because it is reasonable. Hence St. Thomas devotes attention not only to the moral virtues, which are habits of right choice, but also to the intellectual virtue of prudence, which is a habit of judging correctly what the right choice should be. While right choice tends to develop the habit of prudence and wrong choice tends to cloud the moral conscience, men must make the intellectual effort necessary to form a right conscience. Aquinas does not think that virtue is knowledge, but he does think that a man will not be completely virtuous unless he uses whatever brains he has to think out what he ought to do.

§ 8

For St. Thomas's political theory it is natural to refer to the *De Regimine Principum*. This is, however, his work only as far as book II, chapter iv, the rest being added later by Ptolemy of Lucca. It was begun as a manual for the political education of a young Lusignan king of Cyprus, and really offers a less comprehensive notion of St. Thomas's social outlook than the synthesis of law in the *Prima Secundae*. It is on this latter that we shall base ourselves.

Aquinas begins characteristically by insisting on the

[1] *S. Th.* Ia. IIae, qu. 19, art. x.

rational character of law. For, law in general being a rule of action, whether positive or negative, it is primarily a dictate of reason, to which it belongs to adjudicate in the order of means and ends. If law is rightful and therefore genuine law, it is willed and enforced because it is reasonable. Hence the rational character of genuine law is central and primary, and law can be defined as "an ordinance of reason for the common good, promulgated by one who has charge of the community".[1]

This brings St. Thomas at once to the ultimate source of law, for the whole universe forms a community in the charge of its Creator. The history of the universe is the working out of the plan of the creative mind of God. Consequently the divine wisdom, in so far as it governs all activities and changes, is an eternal law.[2] Everything else which can be called by the name of law must in some sense be derived from the eternal law, which is in itself no other than the mind of God.

When, therefore, we speak of the laws of nature, this is not a mere metaphor. The constancies in the physical world which follow upon the natures of existent things reflect the divine mind which eternally contemplates these things as possible. Moreover, it depends upon the divine will that precisely these things should exist and, by fulfilling their natural tendencies, co-operate in the course of history which God decrees. Purely material things have no power of choice and co-operate blindly; created minds, endowed with free will, are able to yield or to refuse co-operation with the divine

[1] *S. Th.* Ia. IIae, qu. 90, art. iv.
[2] *S. Th.* Ia. IIae, qu. 93, art. i.

plan. If they refuse, the divine plan will not thereby be frustrated, for evil wills are brought into the scheme of divine justice, but in the first instance they are faced with a rule of action which they can obey or not. This is natural law in the sense of natural moral law, which is the participation of the eternal law by a rational creature.[1]

There is a parallel between the workings of the speculative and those of the practical reason. In the speculative order there are certain general principles of reason which everyone explicitly or implicitly accepts, but the possibility of disagreement and error emerges and increases as more specific questions are reached. So, in the moral order, the more general imperatives which no one can fail to see, although some may refuse to admit, are contrasted with specific duties about which there may be divergence of opinion from age to age and among individuals in the same age. Truth, nevertheless, is one, and the right application of reason can remove disagreement and error in either sphere. Just as there can be an ascertained body of speculative knowledge, so there can be a true and detailed moral philosophy. Ethical thinking, however, still has a difficulty of its own, for in particular cases it is concerned not with the simple application of a general principle but with taking a multitude of factors into account in due proportion.[2]

Natural law is supplemented by positive law, both divine and human. God, having raised man to supernatural life, gives him the divine law, by following

[1] S. Th. Ia. IIae, qu. 91, art. ii.
[2] Cf. S. Th. Ia. IIae, qu. 94, art. iv.

which he can preserve and foster this life. Upon this divine law depends the authority of the Church, which from time to time makes human laws for the furtherance of the same spiritual aim. This belongs to St. Thomas's theology rather than to his philosophy, but we may remark that, in spite of the occasional exaggerations of mediaeval Churchmen in the heat of controversy, the essential claim by the Church in the middle ages to supremacy in its own spiritual sphere had historically a great deal to do with the recognition that the powers of the state should rightfully be regarded as limited, and with the attempt to discern what their limits should be. Correspondingly, the political side of the Reformation represents a totalitarian attempt by the state to dominate the spiritual realm and to set up new churches which were its creation, and this has helped in modern times to weight the scales in favour of a conception of the state as possessing unlimited powers in every sphere.

With the consideration of those human positive laws which are the laws of states, we arrive at last at the political theory of St. Thomas. Some laws are concerned only with detailing and enforcing the prescriptions of natural law; these should be the same everywhere, and so belong to what in the middle ages was called *ius gentium*, which is not international law but the common internal law of nations. Other laws determine, where uniformity is desirable, alternatives left open by natural law; these are positive laws in the full sense of the term. Thus, says Aquinas by way of example, it rests with positive law to settle what pains and penalties should be inflicted for different varieties of crimes. Both these kinds of law, however, derive their validity from natural law. The one kind is merely a set of conclusions to be drawn from it; the other depends upon the natural law leaving alternatives open and upon the natural good of society demanding that uniformity should be introduced.[1] Positive laws made in violation of these maxims are, for St. Thomas, not laws at all—*magis sunt violentiae quam leges.* In some cases it may be the lesser evil to obey them for the sake of peace; in other cases a stand must be made for principle.[2] In no case, however, do unjust laws carry any obligation of themselves; a doctrine of the juridical omnipotence of parliament would certainly have cut no ice with Aquinas.

St. Thomas wants a reign of law which shall be stable, for he points out that the change of custom brought about by a change of law is a social disturbance of sufficient importance to demand to be compensated by the evident utility of new legislation.[3] The differences of individual cases are such that a certain elasticity must be permitted in the administration of law, but this is a power not to be lightly used.[4] All the time the emphasis is on a stable reign of law whose principles are common to the whole human race.

Asking what is the scope of political legislation, Aquinas proceeds gradually in assigning its due limits. To the question whether human law should restrain all kinds of vice, he replies first that a legislative attempt to repress all evil-doing would defeat its own purpose as being impossible of realization among men as they are.

[1] Cf. *S. Th.* Ia. IIae, qu. 95, art. ii.
[2] Cf. *S. Th.* Ia. IIae, qu. 96, art. iv.
[3] Cf. *S. Th.* Ia. IIae, qu. 97, art. ii.
[4] Cf. *S. Th.* Ia. IIae, qu. 97, art. iv.

Hence law should be concerned only with major evils and, he adds in a clause whose meaning is expanded in the sequel, mainly those which result in harm to other people and which, if left to take their course, would make it impossible to preserve order in human society.[1] In the next article he inquires whether human law should prescribe every kind of good act. He replies that in one sense there is no kind of virtue which may not be required of the citizen, but that a virtuous act may be demanded of him by law only when it is called for by the common good.[2] This opinion becomes still clearer in a later passage, where he states that "human law is ordained for the sake of civil society, which is that of men in their mutual relations. But the mutual relations of men arise from the external acts by which men affect one another. Now this reciprocity of action belongs to the sphere of justice, which is the proper norm of human society. Therefore human law does not prescribe acts other than those of justice, and, if it prescribes acts of other virtues, it does this only in so far as they assume the nature of justice".[3] Thus Aquinas finally assigns to political legislation the sphere of justice, cutting off from it not only the affairs of the spiritual community but also those of private and individual life. The principle of the due liberty of the citizen has attained expression.

There remains to inquire who is to be the political legislator. The state of civil society is natural and requires no contract, however implicit, to bring it about.

[1] Cf. *S. Th.* Ia. IIae, qu. 96, art. ii.
[2] Cf. *S. Th.* Ia. IIae, qu. 96, art. iii.
[3] *S. Th.* Ia. IIae, qu. 100, art. ii.

But it is not the same with the institution of any particular form of government; it cannot be said that any man is naturally designated as the leader and monarch. The right of any particular holder of political power is founded upon the consent of the people, and remains with him as long as he devotes himself to the good of the community as a whole. "To make laws belongs either to the whole people or to some public person who has the care of the whole people."[1] While there are many legitimate forms of constitution, the best will seek to combine the advantages of all forms traditionally enumerated. "Such is a constitution in which there is an apt mixture of monarchy, in so far as there is one supreme ruler; of aristocracy, in so far as many share in power according to their deserts; and of democracy or popular rule, in so far as the rulers can be chosen from the people and are chosen by the people."[2]

Such is St. Thomas's political theory, the system of the free citizen in the limited state. In modern times it is rightly associated with the practice and example of England, but it is of very great interest to see that it has its roots in the middle ages and in the work of St. Thomas Aquinas.

[1] *S. Th.* Ia. IIae, qu. 90, art. iii.
[2] *S. Th.* Ia. IIae, qu. 105, art. i.

CHAPTER VII

DUNS SCOTUS

§ 1

IN passing at once from Aquinas to Scotus we are preserving the scale of an introduction by omitting a number of important thinkers of the second rank, such as Henry of Ghent, Richard of Middleton and Giles of Rome. The true figure of Duns Scotus is only now beginning to emerge again. By the attribution to him of several works which are really of the school of Ockham, he had come to seem the precursor of the disruption of mediaeval thought. The patient labours of a number of Franciscan scholars in sifting his genuine works from the spurious have placed him in an entirely different light. He is no mere destructive critic but a systematic thinker in the grand manner, second only to St. Thomas in the middle ages, and presenting another synthesis of Augustine and Aristotle.

John Duns the Scotsman was born about 1270, became a Franciscan, lectured at Oxford and at Paris, and died prematurely in 1308. His principal works are the two commentaries on the *Sentences* of Peter Lombard, called from their places of origin the *Opus Oxoniense* and the *Reportata Parisiensia;* mention must also be made of the brief disquisition *De Primo Principio*. The *De Rerum Principio*, however, is an earlier product of the thirteenth-century Franciscan school, while the *Theoremata* and the *Grammatica Speculativa* are instances of the logic-chopping of a later period, when the views of Ockham were in the ascendant.

On many questions Scotus is less thoroughly Aristotelian than Aquinas. Aquinas had adopted the Aristotelian principle that the natural object of the human intellect was the being of sensible things; Scotus, in conscious opposition, maintains that every intellect as such is capable of apprehending the whole range of being (*omnis intellectus est totius entis communissime sumpti*). Yet the opposition is not so violent when we see what each meant in detail. The test application is in the theory of the mode of knowledge belonging to the disembodied soul after death. Here the new Aristotelianism, with its insistence on the natural unity of body and soul, had raised a problem. Henry of Ghent went to the length of asserting that the disembodied soul could obtain new knowledge only by a miraculous infusion. Aquinas is much more moderate. As the soul can exist without the body, so it is in that state capable of the activity of pure thought which is appropriate to a spiritual being. Although such a mode of knowledge is in itself superior to the kind of thinking which draws its material from sensation, it is not naturally available to the disembodied soul with the clearness and distinctness which would make it a complete substitute for terrestrial experience. Nevertheless, however imperfect a spirit it may be, the soul after death is in natural communication with other spirits.[1]

Scotus admits that in our present condition the primary adequate object of the human intellect is the being of sensible things. But this, he says, is not due to

[1] Cf. St. Thomas Aquinas: *Summa Theologica* I, qu. 89, art. i.

the nature of the intellect as such, nor does it even follow simply from the union of body and soul. It is a fact that our present knowledge results from the co-operation of our sensible and intellectual faculties, but this seems to be no more than a contingent and preparatory stage of human nature. The soul, when disembodied at death, will begin to act naturally as a pure intellect and, even when reunited with the body, will not lose the power of purely spiritual communication which is, after all, the natural prerogative of every intellect.[1] That is the real extent of his disagreement with Aquinas on this question. It is more than a difference of emphasis, but it is not a radical opposition.

§ 2

With this confidence in the efficacy of intellect Scotus approaches the problem of the relation between the structure of thought and the structure of fact. The Abelardian theory of abstraction had left this somewhat obscure; Scotus takes the matter up again and, following a tendency observable among some of the earlier thirteenth-century Franciscans, makes a much debated contribution to its clarification. This is the celebrated theory of the formal distinction.

The validity of abstract thought had been asserted by Abelard in the formula that one factor was considered separately from another but not as really separate from it. The mental activity of abstraction operated upon fact in such a way as to isolate elements which did not really exist in isolation. Hence the

[1] Cf. *Opus Oxoniense* I, dist. 3, qu. 3, no. 24; IV, dist 45, qu. 2, no. 12.

content of universal concepts was real, while their form of universality came from the mind.

The distinction, then, between factors thus isolated by abstraction was not a real distinction; it was made by the mind, but it had a foundation in fact. Evidently another question remained to be asked, and it was asked by Scotus. What was this foundation in fact? What could be the foundation in fact for a distinction if it was not some sort of distinction which itself belonged to the realm of fact? It was not in the full sense a real distinction, a distinction between things. Nevertheless Scotus could not acquiesce in the ambiguous designation of a distinction of reason with foundation in fact. He preferred to speak of a formal non-identity or distinction, a cleavage less radical than a real distinction but more than a mere distinction of reason.

Scotus seeks to draw up a list of the varying degrees of unity and the corresponding degrees of distinction. The loosest kind of unity is a mere unity of aggregation, in which things happen to be together, or to be thought of together, but there is no structural principle which makes them an intelligible unity. Such is a heap of stones or, to take a modern example, the heterogeneous collection of objects to be found in a surrealist picture, when the onlooker simply wonders how on earth they came to be in the artist's mind at the same time.

The next kind of unity is unity of order, in which different things are connected by some intelligible principle of structure. Such is in the realm of thought the unity of a series, and in the realm of fact the unity of a house or a machine. Then comes the unity of qualification (*unitas per accidens*), in which one factor, though not necessarily connected with another, never-theless determines it and makes one thing with it. Thus, when I am thinking, my thoughts are, although transi-tory, genuine determinations of myself and make one thing with me. Still closer is the unity of essential principles, such as matter and form, related as poten-tiality and actuality (*unitas per se compositi ex prin-cipiis essentialibus per se actu et per se potentia*). Such a unity cannot be dissolved without the thing itself ceasing to be.

A fifth kind of unity is described as the unity of simplicity. This is a genuine identity, in which factors are not merely united but are really one. In a thought, act and content are no more than distinguishable ele-ments in one simple event. Yet we do not mean the same by an act of thinking and the content of a thought. However true it is that act and content are really one, the distinction between them is not altogether made by me; it is presented to me, and I perceive it in fact. It is in such cases that Scotus speaks of formal non-identity. It is not until formal meaning (*ratio formalis*) is the same that it becomes possible to speak of the most absolute kind of unity which is formal identity.[1]

This theory of the formal distinction became a typical thesis of the Scotistic school and was attacked with equal determination by the representatives of the other scholastic traditions. It was alleged to be a confusion between the structure of thought and the structure of fact. It was held that there followed from it a real identity of different instances of the same universal, so

[1] Cf. *Op. Oxon.* I, dist 2, qu. 7, nn. 42-4.

that humanity in Peter and humanity in Paul was in some sense the same thing. Scotus, however, was sufficiently careful to contrast formal identity with real identity, and it cannot be denied that he was attempting to answer a legitimate question provoked by the abstract and analytic character of thinking. His view cannot be left out of account when we are seeking a just conception of the relationship between thought and fact.

§ 3

Scotus has a theory of being very different from that of Aquinas, or perhaps it would be more exact to say that he gives a very different meaning to the terms *esse* and *ens*. Being is, for him, simply the most universal and the poorest in content of all notions. It is precisely on this ground that Scotus adheres to the common formula that being is not a genus. For it is not a positive residue left after all the differentiations of being have been removed by conceptual abstraction; rather it has no positive content and is equivalent to what is not nothing (*Se extendit ad quodcumque quod non est nihil*).

This concept of being is strictly one in all its applications. Hence, in opposition to the Thomists, Scotus asserts that being is univocal, defining an univocal concept as one whose unity is sufficient to involve contradiction if it is both affirmed and denied of the same subject.[1] The opposition is more verbal than real. For, if an univocal concept is defined in this way, St. Thomas would have no difficulty in admitting that what he

[1] Cf. *Op. Oxon.* I, dist. 3, qu. 2, no. 5.

meant by being is univocal. Moreover, being as Scotus understood it is univocal in every sense.

From the Thomistic point of view it might be said that the Scotistic notion of being belongs altogether to the side of essence as opposed to that of existence. To be a being means simply to have an essence of some sort. It is only a logical consequence, therefore, when Scotus denies the distinction of essence and existence. *Simpliciter falsum est quod esse sit aliud ab essentia.*[1] It must then be admitted that Scotus did not grasp what Aquinas was about in his theory of being, and it might be supposed that there was an enormous lacuna in his metaphysic. In the end, however, he reaches a metaphysic not far removed from that of St. Thomas; this is because the place left vacant by the Thomistic notion of existence is filled by the new concept of thisness (*haecceitas*).

For Scotus recognizes that all the elements which he has hitherto revealed, all that can be attributed to things, including being itself as he understands it, are of themselves universal. The individuality of real things is not yet accounted for. Hence, beyond all that in reality corresponds with universals or combinations of universals, he claims that things exhibit a principle of individuality, a thisness, which is not reducible to any other factor. "The singular adds an entity over and above the entity of the universal. Consequently the apprehension of the universal is not the complete ground of an apprehension of the singular adequate to the whole knowability of the singular."[2]

[1] *Op. Oxon.* IV, dist. 13, qu. 1, no. 38.
[2] *Op. Oxon.* IV, dist. 9, qu. 2, no. 10.

Thisness is not a universal like other universals, for it is precisely the principle of individuality. The thisness of this is by its very notion different from the thisness of that. *Haecceitas est de se haec.*[1] The understanding of a thing is complete when we have not only fully analysed it in universal terms but have perceived these factors as belonging to something which is this. Hence understanding attains to the singular and has finished its task only when it has attained the singular.

The parallel between the Thomistic notion of existence and the Scotistic notion of thisness should be obvious. Both these great metaphysicians decline to lose themselves in abstractions, but lead us back to the real world by an emphasis on the individuality of the existent. Scotus brings out very forcibly the unique character of individuality. Nevertheless we miss in him the recognition of the fundamental identity of individuality and existence which is the distinguishing mark of the metaphysic of Aquinas.

§ 4

Having thus noticed the principal innovations of Scotus, we can glance at the rest of his system, observing what effect they have upon it. His conception of matter, like that of St. Bonaventure and the earlier scholastics, belongs more to physics than to metaphysics. First matter is what is in common to all material things and, although it is not in fact to be discovered without form, there is no absolute reason why it should not exist separately.

[1] *Rep. Paris.* II, dist. 12, qu. 5, no. 8.

Scotus criticizes the Thomistic view of matter as pure potentiality in the order of essence. Matter, he says, cannot have simply the objective potentiality of what might exist but does not exist. For it is an element in real things, part of the object of the divine creative activity, and the persistent subject of substantial change. Such a factor must have the subjective potentiality of something which is itself real but is capable of further determination. It is described simply as potentiality because it is the least actual of entities, being in potentiality to all forms, substantial and accidental, but it is already, although in the humblest possible way, an actual reality in itself. There is no greater difficulty in supposing two actual realities in a composite thing than there is in supposing that a composite thing exists at all. In other words, Scotus rejects the Thomistic conception of first matter on the ground that it is unintelligible and reducible to nonentity.[1]

With this view of a composite entity it is possible to preserve the natural notion of an organism as possessing a hierarchy of substantial forms. These forms are received successively in the process of development of a living thing, and they disappear gradually in the process of its decomposition. The dead body of an animal still retains for a time the corporeal forms which constituted the proximate disposition for the reception of its vital principle. Hence the spiritual soul of man, which must be attributed to the creative activity of God, is the principle of life, of sensation and of thought, but presupposes an organized body, which is the proper product of the generative activity of the parents.

[1] Cf. *Op. Oxon.* II, dist. 12, qu. 1, nn. 10-1ₑ.

The spiritual character of thought is immediately evident to anyone who reflects on his act of thinking. *Quilibet enim experitur in se intelligere ; et experitur in se, quando intelligit, quandum operationem quae non est alicuius organi.*[1] For matter is essentially divisible or voluminous, while the act of thinking is introspectively known to be simple and indivisible. It is equally plain by reflection that the act of thinking belongs to the individual man, so that the theory of Averroes that thinking is the work in us of a separate and impersonal intellect must be rejected with contumely as *vilissimus et irrationabilissimus inter errores omnes philosophorum.*

Scotus assigns a certain primacy to the will over the intellect, but the common contrast between the alleged voluntarism of Scotus and the intellectualism of Aquinas is a rather artificial antithesis. It amounts more to a personal preference in consideration than to an abstract difference of doctrine. As a seventeenth-century writer quaintly puts it, Scotus, "not unmindful of courtesy, behaved respectfully to the intellect".[2] But he likes to think of understanding as leading to volition, so that the will is regarded as the supreme personal activity. While the intellect must wait upon evidence and is constrained by the objects presented to it, the will chooses freely the orientation which the personality gives to itself. Nothing belongs to yourself more completely than your will and its acts.

Scotus, however, is anxious that we should not think

---

[1] *Rep. Paris.* IV, dist. 43, qu. 2, no. 8.
[2] *Comitatis non immemor, erga intellectum officiosum se gessit.* Macedo: *Collationes doctrinae S. Thomae et Scoti, cit. ap.* Longpré: *La Philosophie du B. Duns Scot*, p. 202.

of intellect and will as if they were two agents within us with disparate activities; this, he considers, would be the result of speaking of them as really distinct. Intellect and will are, in fact, one reality with the soul. Nevertheless there is a difference of meaning in the terms designating the faculties of intellect and of will and the essence of the soul itself. Hence the distinction is not purely verbal, but there is room for an application of the theory of the formal distinction. Intellect and will are formally distinct from each other and from the essence of the soul.

§ 5

It has sometimes been said that Scotus betrays hesitations about the validity of the philosophical demonstration of the existence of God, and that his conception of God is one of an arbitrary cosmic will rather than of a supremely rational and benevolent creator and ruler of the universe. Since these accusations are based on the *Theoremata*, which Scotus did not write, they need not be taken into account. His authentic thought on the subject is firm, constructive and well balanced.

He prefers to lay emphasis on the central metaphysical considerations rather than on the Aristotelian proof of the first unmoved mover, which lent a certain imaginative aid to the mediaeval mind in arriving at the existence of God. From any property of an effect which that effect can acquire only from a cause of a certain kind, you can, he says, conclude to the existence of a cause of that kind. Hence the existence of God is demonstrable both in physics or natural philosophy and in metaphysics, physics arriving at an unmoved mover and metaphysics at a first being. The strictly metaphysical proof, however, provides a much more positive knowledge of God, "for it is a more perfect and direct knowledge of the first being to know him as the first being or necessary existent than to know him as the first mover".[1]

The fundamental evidence, then, of the existence of God resides in those characteristics of the objects of experience which are taken into account by the metaphysician. It is because we find that the things around us are manifold, contingent and composite that we are able to see that they must have an ultimate cause which is one, necessary and metaphysically simple. But for Scotus the hallmark of contingency is to be discovered in being finite; infinity is the most essential characteristic which thought must attribute to the necessary being.

Infinity can be defined in two ways. In itself it is such that nothing of entity is wanting to it which can be found together in one being; in relation to finite beings it is such that it transcends them not by some determinate proportion but beyond any proportion which can be determined.[2] This infinity of being is the privilege of God. Like Aquinas, then, Scotus arrives at an *ens infinitum,* but, while for Aquinas the stress is on *ens,* for Scotus it is on *infinitum.* In the philosophy of St. Thomas, God is infinite being because he is being itself; with Scotus's different and more restricted notion

---

[1] *Op. Oxon.,* Prol., qu. 2, no. 21. Cf. *In Met.* I, qu. 1, no. 35.
[2] Cf. *Quodlibet* V, no. 4.

of being, the mode of infinity demands the chief attention and provides the metaphysical impetus.

In speaking of God as *ipsum esse,* too, Scotus shows another verbal coincidence with St. Thomas, but the later philosopher understands the formula as meaning rather the fullness of essence, the sum of all perfections. It is the nature of such a being to exist, whatever else may exist or not exist. Hence its very notion, provided that this can be seen to be self-consistent, is a guarantee of its existence. Here Scotus finds a justification for the argument of St. Anselm.

The infinite being can only be a spiritual being, since a material thing is essentially a finite quantum divisible into finite parts. Consequently the divine life is the supreme activity of intelligence and will. God's will is altogether in harmony with his intelligence—*Deus rationabilissime vult.* Hence, in the logical order, the first motion of God's will is towards himself as the supreme value, the second towards the creation of persons who will be able to love him in their degree, and the third towards the creation of the means which those persons will require. Scotus sees in the decree of creation not only the divine goodness ungrudgingly diffusing itself but the desire of a person for other persons who will enter with him into communion of love—*Deus vult habere alios diligentes.*[1]

Created things partially reflect the perfection of the creator, and the unity of order in the universe reflects the unity of simplicity in God. God enjoys a threefold primacy. As first in the order of causes he is the most completely actual being, containing virtually every

[1] *Op. Oxon.* III, dist. 32, qu. 1, no. 6.

possible kind of actuality; as first in the order of ends he is the highest value, containing virtually every possible kind of value; as first in the order of eminence he is the most perfect being, containing transcendently every possible kind of perfection.[1] With such a being it must be the most real desire of a created person to enter into communion, and Scotus, like Aquinas, is ready to speak of a natural desire to enter into the fullest possible intimacy with God, although the fulfilment of this desire must depend upon the will of God to communicate himself and is, therefore, supernatural.

Such is the third of the great thirteenth-century metaphysical systems. St. Bonaventure, although deeply affected by the rediscovery of Aristotle, had deliberately kept as closely as he could to the tradition of St. Augustine. St. Thomas Aquinas, basing himself wholeheartedly on Aristotelian principles, showed that the new philosophy was capable of reconquering the religious conclusions of the old. Duns Scotus occupies something of an intermediate position, liking to follow Bonaventure but taking a considerably more Aristotelian line. St. Thomas is undoubtedly the greatest of the three, and his system is the closest-knit and most comprehensive, but those who are sympathetic with scholastic thought will want also to consult the others, and metaphysical thinking would be considerably impoverished if it were deprived of the contributions of St. Bonaventure and of Duns Scotus.

[1] *De Primo Principio*, c. 3, no. 11.

CHAPTER VIII

THE FOURTEENTH AND FIFTEENTH CENTURIES

§ 1

IT will have been impossible to follow a history of mediaeval philosophy so far without a sense of the continuity of scholastic thought. There was not a succession of individualistic thinkers, each determined to create an entirely new system without regard to what others had said; rather philosophy progressed by a gradual accumulation of detail accompanied by criticism and emendation as the occasion called for them. There comes a time in such a process when more radical criticism is useful in order to throw out any lumber that remains and to lead men once again to examine their presuppositions. When the thirteenth century, with its imposing syntheses of thought, had come to an end, it was natural that a critical period should follow. Unfortunately scholasticism was disastrously less well served by its critics than by its leading positive exponents. The influence of William of Ockham and his followers almost succeeded in burying the thirteenth-century achievement under a dead weight of verbal logic which offered no mental sustenance.

Before Ockham, however, and among the contemporaries of Scotus, there appears a predominantly critical mind whose rather indiscriminate desire to simplify matters and get down to brass tacks nevertheless deserves respectful attention. This is Durandus de Sancto Porciano, whose personality, in so far as it can be resuscitated from his now neglected pages, seems to be somewhat of the type of a mediaeval Locke. He was born about 1270 at Saint-Pourçain-sur-Sioule, became a Dominican, taught at Paris until he was made *lector sancti palatii* at the court of Clement V and John XXII at Avignon, was successively bishop of Limoux, of Le Puy, and of Meaux, and died in 1334.

According to the researches of Koch, there were three redactions of his principal work, a commentary on the *Sentences*. In the first version his innovations are most apparent, but these aroused the violent opposition of his brother Dominicans, who were beginning to adopt as their common doctrine the teaching of Aquinas. Hence Durandus, in deference to their objections, produced a second edition, in which his personal views were very much toned down. Finally, when he became a bishop and was released from the discipline of his order, he revised his work once again and brought it closer to its original form, although without returning completely to the opinions which had been attacked. It was this third edition which was printed several times in the sixteenth century, but no edition has been published since that of Venice in 1586. Among his other works are a number of *Quodlibets*, two *Quaestiones Disputatae* and a *Tractatus de Habitibus*. A complete printed edition of his works has not yet appeared.

The principle known to later times as Ockham's razor, which states that entities are not to be multiplied without necessity, is in fact to be found in a great number of mediaeval writers, including St. Thomas, but in no one is its tendency more evident than in Durandus. He seems to be something of an empiricist, never being happy to admit the reality of anything which is not pretty obvious in experience, and he has some of the defects of the empiricist, failing to notice all that experience offers and to exhaust its implications.

In order that sensation should take place, he says, nothing else is required but the affection of the sense-organ by the sensible object.[1] Given the power of vision and a visible object with a suitable relation between them, the act of vision occurs, and there is no need to talk about *species* as representing the external object.[2] In the first version of his work Durandus considers even the cognitive act to be simply a relation between the mind and its object, but he does not return to this extreme simplification in his final version. In dealing with thought he will never admit a concept or *verbum mentis* distinct from the act of thinking—*verbum est ipsemet actus intelligendi*.[3]

Durandus, then, regards the cognitive faculty as fully equipped to produce its act as soon as its object is suitably presented to it. Hence the difference between ways of knowing is exclusively due to the manner in which the object is presented to the mind. This seems to be the reason why he denies that habits can properly be said to belong to the intellect, and asserts that they belong rather to the organs through which the material of thought is presented. "Every modification of a cognitive faculty", he says, "depends in the first place on the manner of presentation of the object of which the knowledge is in question, and repetition brings

[1] *In. II Sent.*, dist. 13, qu. 2, no. 10.
[2] *In. II Sent.*, dist. 3, qu. 6, no. 21.
[3] *In. I Sent.*, dist. 27, qu. 1, no. 26.

about facility in similar presentations. When a modification due to the first presentation of an object is fortified by repetition, there remains not merely this modification but a facility in making a similar presentation. This being given on the part of the presentation, there is a corresponding modification and facility on the part of the intellect, whose intrinsic nature it is to be modified by its object, and which of itself lacks no disposition required for any act, since it is like a blank tablet."[1]

The desire of Durandus to reduce as much as possible to the category of relation becomes fully intelligible when we meet with his metaphysical thesis that, while a relation is in a certain sense distinct from its foundation, it is not so distinct as to be in metaphysical composition with it. A subject of relations is one thing with its relations. The kind of distinction which Durandus here admits seems to be exactly parallel with the formal distinction of Scotus.

That Durandus was guilty of oversimplification is fairly evident. Nevertheless his criticism was of a healthy kind, and should have called forth a useful re-examination of fundamental concepts. His opponents, however, do not appear to have been of a sufficient calibre for more than negative polemic. The critical movement which actually established itself and maintained its influence until the end of the middle ages was of a less healthy sort. This was the nominalism or terminism of William of Ockham and his disciples.

[1] *Tractatus de Habitibus*, qu. 4, art. 8, *cit. ap.* J. Koch: *Durandus de S. Porciano*, pp. 141-2.

§ 2

The pleasant village of Ockham in Surrey possesses no memorial of its most famous son, whose birth falls probably within the last decade of the thirteenth century. William of Ockham became a Franciscan and studied at Oxford, but he never proceeded beyond the degree of bachelor or *inceptor,* whence he came to be known by his followers as the *venerabilis inceptor.* In 1324 his subversive theories caused him to be delated to Pope John XXII at Avignon, but the Holy See did not find sufficient evidence to justify a condemnation. Soon afterwards, however, William became a supporter of the German emperor-elect, Lewis of Bavaria, in his political activities against the papacy; the later writings of Ockham are mainly concerned with the relations of Church and state. He died about 1348, leaving behind him the regulation commentary on the *Sentences,* some *Quodlibets,* a *Summa Totius Logicae* and a commentary on Aristotle's logic under the name of *Expositio Aurea super totam artem veterem.* If mild flippancy be not out of place, these logical writings might well be recommended to the Mouse in *Alice in Wonderland* as a more effective substitute for the driest thing he knew, but their historical importance forbids us to neglect them.

As we have seen, one of the mainsprings of mediaeval philosophy was the discussion of the relation between the structure of thought and the structure of fact, which first appeared as the controversy about universals in the eleventh and twelfth centuries. The theory of Abelard, sound as far as it went, left another question to be raised. Scotus raised this question and, with his theory of the formal distinction, solved it in the sense of a close correspondence between the structure of thought and the structure of fact; logic and metaphysics were brought into the most intimate connection. The philosophy of Ockham is at the opposite extreme; logic and metaphysics are almost completely dissociated.

The source of this dissociation is to be found in the theory of the cognitive act as a natural sign of its object. Instead of interpreting language in terms of thought, Ockham interprets thought on the analogy of language. While words are conventional signs of things, cognitive acts are to be considered as natural signs; according to the nature of mind they point to and stand for (*supponunt pro*) the objects of knowledge. The relationship between knowledge and fact seems to have become wholly external. Nevertheless Ockham maintains an acquaintance with the singular, which is a contact of mind with concrete reality, but he is ready to compromise the objectivity of the universal concept. The universal is not an awareness of a factor in reality, but stands in some vague way for the sum of things of which it can be predicated. The sciences, as organized systems of universals, are really about concepts rather than about things.

Consistently with all this, Ockham rejects the doctrine of *species* and the distinction between the active and the passive function of intellect. With so dubious a relation between thought and fact, it is not surprising that many hitherto accepted metaphysical theses become less than certain. Since only the individual thing is real in any sense, the analysis of a thing into essence and existence, substance and attribute, is a merely conceptual elaboration which cannot be transported into the structure of the thing itself. An infinite series of causes is an impossibility for thought, but it does not follow that it is an impossibility in fact. Hence the classical demonstration of the existence of God is compromised.

Ockham finds the type of reality in personal will; it is the power of self-determination which is the essence of the self. His conception of God is, consequently, of a supreme and arbitrary will, contingently decreeing what his creatures should do and what they should avoid. We have no right to attribute to the Creator our human notions of good and evil. and so all morality is a positive theological code.

The extremes to which such a system could lead were shown by Nicholas of Autrecourt, who has been described by Rashdall as a mediaeval Hume. It appears from his condemnation by Clement VI in 1347 that he held no proposition to be evident or demonstrable unless it could be reduced to the principle of contradiction. Therefore, like Hume, he maintained that the existence of one thing could never entail the existence of another. The notion of causation being thus overturned, the existence of God could not be philosophically established. We could not be sure even that the things which in experience appear to exist really do exist. In the end, we are left, like Hume again, with a succession of mental phenomena and nothing more.

John of Mirecourt was condemned for similar opinions at much the same time. The terminist school in general, however, remained within the bounds of theological orthodoxy, but devoted their chief attention to those verbal gymnastics which at a later period gave scholasticism a bad name. A comparison between Ockham and the terminists on the one hand and Carnap and the Vienna circle on the other might be worth the while of some writer to draw out at length.

§ 3

We have already mentioned that Ockham devoted his last years to political controversy on the side of the emperor against the Pope. The fourteenth century was, indeed, a period of ferment in political thought and activity. The rise of the national state was beginning to endanger the mediaeval equilibrium.

Classical political theory, as we find it in Plato and Aristotle, was implicitly totalitarian. It was totalitarian in so far as no sphere of human life was excluded from the sphere of legislation; it was implicitly so, because the full consequences of such a principle had not been considered or experienced, and no alternative had yet come to mind. At any rate the Roman imperial system acknowledged no limitation, and it was natural that, as soon as the Christian Church was relieved from persecution and recognized by the state, it had at once to face interference by the state in its own proper affairs.

In the East, where the Roman system persisted at Byzantium, the emperor eventually detached his subjects from the unity of the Church and brought Byzantine Christianity under state domination. When the West relapsed into anarchy, the unity of the Church was guaranteed by the papacy, and, as order was restored, the new states grew up under the guardianship of the Church. The stability of mediaeval order depended upon the equilibrium of the claims of Church and of state. The main interest of the middle ages for general political theory lies in the fact that, in the process of deciding what was the legitimate sphere of the Church and what the sphere of the state, men were led to try to define more precisely what was the function of the state within the secular sphere. We have already seen that, in the philosophy of St. Thomas Aquinas, this was defined as the prosecution of justice, and it left room for a private and individual life over which the state had no jurisdiction. Similarly, in contrast with the Church, the human origin of political sovereignty was stated and emphasized, and it became common doctrine that, although the institution of civil society and authority belonged to the law of nature which was the law of God, nevertheless the actual secular rulers owed their authority in some way to designation by the people. That is why Lord Acton could describe St. Thomas as the first Whig.

In the earlier middle ages there had been frequent conflict between the spiritual universalism of the Church and the secular universalism of the empire, which had been renewed in Charlemagne and his successors. In theory the two were to co-operate in harmony; in practice they were often at loggerheads. After the death of Frederick II in the middle of the thirteenth century, imperial universalism was no longer in a position to threaten the freedom of the Church, although the ideal of a universal empire sprang to life again for a brief moment with Henry VII at the beginning of the fourteenth century, and received its literary monument in Dante's attempt to delimit the spheres of universal Church and universal state in the *De Monarchia*.

Meanwhile the rising and more dangerous opponent of the unity of Christendom and the freedom of the Church was the national state. From the time of Philip Augustus, France had become more unified and centralized, and it was the troops of Philip the Fair, a century afterwards, who manhandled in Boniface VIII the personification of the rights of the Church. The opposition of Lewis of Bavaria to the papacy was no longer the opposition of a universal empire but the opposition of a German monarch. It is in this context of rising nationalism that we have to see the new political theories of the fourteenth century.

The amount of novelty contained in these has sometimes been exaggerated. The impassioned supporters of king or emperor did not venture to deny the popular origin of secular sovereignty; the doctrine of the divine right of kings came into prominence only among certain theorists at the period of the Reformation. When democratic ideas were expounded, as by Marsilius of Padua, these were merely a development of thirteenth-century views such as we find in St. Thomas Aquinas. What was really new was a totalitarian tendency, an assertion of the complete independence and omnicompetence of the secular state.

The jurists of Philip the Fair, of whom the most important was John of Paris, the author of a treatise *De Potestate Regia et Papali*, drew as closely as possible the bounds of the spiritual sphere of the Church, and regarded all the temporal rights of the Church as due to a revocable concession from the secular ruler. John, at the same time, took the opportunity of preaching the superiority of the self-sufficient national state to a universal empire and reign of law.

Among the supporters of Lewis of Bavaria were John of Jandun, William of Ockham and, most celebrated of all, Marsilius of Padua. Marsilius, in the *Defensor Pacis* (1324-6), developed in the interests of his imperial patron a theory that all power in Church and state was derived from the people. While the preparation of laws must be confided to a small number of experts, it is within the competence of the people, or at any rate of the better sort (*pars valentior*), to decide whether these should pass into act. Then it is the business of the government, whether it consist of a single ruler or of an aristocracy or of a democracy, to carry the will of the people into effect. The people are the source of un-limited authority both in Church and in state, and indeed Marsilius attributes to law a power of regulation over the whole field of human life which would leave in principle no room for individual liberty. The clergy, especially, are to become servants of the state and to be financially dependent upon it.

All these notions were to have regrettable conse-quences at a later period and down to our own time. In the fourteenth century we witness the beginning of the collapse of mediaeval civilization and the rise of some of the less fortunate elements in the modern world.

§ 4

Meanwhile, in general philosophy, the fourteenth and fifteenth centuries were also a period of decline. The influence of terminism tended to reduce philosophical inquiry to barren exercises in dialectic. The Dominicans continued to follow Aquinas, and the Franciscans Scotus, but they added little to them. The Thomists, however, included a famous commentator in John Capreolus (c. 1380-1444), the author of the *Defensiones Theologiae Divi Thomae,* and a famous moralist in St. Antoninus, archbishop of Florence (c. 1389-1459), who wrote penetratingly on the application of ethical principles to economic life. But it must be admitted that this was, on the whole, an age of commentators with little of their own to say; their small originalities of detail do not claim attention in a rapid survey of this kind.

Nor need the dreary efforts of the terminists detain us, except that, perhaps for the very reason that their method of philosophizing was essentially sterile, some of them began to turn their attention to the kind of investigation out of which developed the modern experimental sciences. John Buridan (d. c. 1358) is known in strict philosophy for his inquiries into the nature of volition, in which he could not see his way out of a psychological determinism, making the will yield always to the strongest attraction of the moment. The celebrated example of Buridan's ass, dying of starvation because unable to make up its mind between two equal and equidistant bundles of hay, is, although it is not to be found in his works, a fair enough statement of a difficulty arising from his system. He was happier, however, in the region of physics. He criticized the Aristotelian theories of natural place and of the intelligences which brought about motion in the heavenly bodies, and explained motion instead through an impetus which was communicated by the source of the motion and continued until neutralized by resistance. He thus anticipated part of Newton's physics.

Nicholas of Oresme, bishop of Lisieux (d. 1382), suggested the possibility that the earth rotated round the sun rather than the sun round the earth. He was also known in his day as a financial expert, and wrote a treatise *De Origine, Natura, Jure et Mutationibus Monetarum*. In this work he first enunciated the principle about bad money driving good out of circulation which we usually call Gresham's law.

Another scientifically-minded terminist was Albert of Saxony, bishop of Halberstadt (*c.* 1316-90), who inclined to accept Buridan's theory of impetus in place of the Aristotelian doctrine of motion. He commented critically upon the *Physics*, the *De Caelo et Mundo* and the *De Generatione et Corruptione* of Aristotle. Here, then, in the fourteenth century too, we find the first hints of a period when the experimental sciences would overshadow pure philosophy in the estimation of the majority of men.

§ 5

There remains to be mentioned yet one more current of philosophical thinking. That the middle ages were an eminently religious epoch is obvious, and the mediaeval attitude towards the central doctrines of religion was eminently rational. Lacking a logic of probability, the men of the middle ages had comparatively little sense of historical evidence, and an embroidery of legend was allowed to gather round matters which were not of primary importance. But, having a clear and highly developed logic of certainty, mediaeval thinkers showed the utmost rigour in discussing and defining those essential points of religious philosophy and of Christian faith where metaphysical acumen finds its rightful application. Yet there is always the type of religious mind which, in Sir Thomas Browne's phrase, loves to pursue its reason to an *O altitudo!* The mystical type of mind is inclined to be impatient of analytical inquiry and elaborate ratiocination. No mediaeval mind could avoid these altogether, but there is in mediaeval philosophy a distinctively mystical current of thought, usually in close relation with the Neoplatonic tradition. The earliest example is John Scotus Erigena. In the later middle ages, as confidence in analytic philosophy decreases, examples grow more frequent.

Already in the thirteenth century, William of Moerbeke, the translator of Aristotle, had also made available in Latin some of the works of Proclus, and these appear to have influenced a number of German Dominicans, like Dietrich of Freiburg and especially Master Eckhart of Hochheim. Dietrich, whose principal work is the *De Intellectu et Intelligibili,* finds room within a Neoplatonic framework for certain Thomistic theses, such as the unity of the substantial form, the notion of first matter as pure potentiality, and the intrinsic possibility of an eternal creation. But the main structure of his philosophy is plainly Neoplatonic, with a gradual emanation from God of pure intelligences, souls and corporeal things, and a corresponding return of created things to God. By the possession of active intellect men are themselves on the level of pure intelligence and can attain the vision of things in God.

Eckhart (d. 1327) wrote both in Latin and in German, and brought his ideas together in Latin in the *Opus Tripartitum*. He makes a curious use of the Thomistic distinction of essence and existence, maintaining that, while everything has its own essence, there is but one existence, which is the existence of God. Since God just is the existence of everything, he is everywhere, and nothing is outside God. Eckhart says that not only the creative act but creation itself is eternal, its real existence being in the divine present. This would seem to lead to a denial of the reality of time. The mystical union of the soul with God does not consist merely in knowledge and love; it is a recognition of unity in the very substance of the soul which is sustained by the divine existence. For this a complete renunciation of creatures and of separate selfhood is prerequisite.

It is not quite clear whether Eckhart meant literally all that he said or his strange utterances are due to an attempt to express the inexpressible. At any rate the strange utterances were condemned in their obvious sense by John XXII in 1329. Nevertheless the influence of Eckhart remained alive in orthodox German Dominican mystics of the fourteenth century, like Henry Seuse (Suso) and John Tauler.

This tradition seems to have persisted in Germany and, at the period of transition from the middle ages to the Renaissance, received a final expression from Nicholas of Cusa, Cardinal and bishop of Brixen (1401-64). Nicholas was a busy churchman as well as a thinker, and a mathematician as well as a theologian and philosopher. His chief philosophical work is the *De Docta Ignorantia,* whose title may be paraphrased as the nescience which transcends knowledge. For Nicholas is convinced that, in order to attain to an apprehension of God, we must go beyond the sphere of the discursive reason, which is governed by the principle of contradiction.

God is the reconciliation of contraries. The first book of the *De Docta Ignorantia* employs a wealth of mathematical analogies to establish the divine paradoxes. God is the supreme unity which is both *maximum absolutum* and *minimum absolutum.* "For maximum in quantity is maximum in magnitude, and minimum in quantity is maximum in littleness. Remove, therefore, maximum and minimum from quantity by abstracting magnitude and littleness, and you will clearly see that maximum and minimum coincide." [1] Not all the dialectic is quite as barefaced as this, but it will serve as an example. So, too, the circumference of an infinite circle would be a straight line, and an infinite straight line would be a triangle, and this triangle would be a circle. Similar considerations are used to illustrate the doctrine of the Trinity. The way to God by affirmation and the way by negation must be used side by side, and in the end their significance is identical.

The second book deals with the created universe as *maximum contractum.* God is in all things and all things are in God, and all things tend again towards unity in God. The human mind, seeking unity in thought, reaches out towards that illumined nescience which transcends analytic knowledge and is union with

[1] *De Docta Ignorantia* I, 4.

God. The means towards this union is Christ, the Incarnate Word, who is both creator and creature; this is the theme of the third book.

Lovers of paradox will find entertainment in Nicholas of Cusa, but to a more prosaic mind these dialectical fireworks are a poor substitute for the sober analytic reasoning of the great thinkers of the thirteenth century. The philosophy of Cusanus is not only astonishing in itself, but it is astonishing that such a system should have been put forward not by some obscure eccentric but by one of the leading European figures of the age. It not merely ignores the kind of philosophy which was still taught at all the universities, but it blithely overlooks the fundamental distinction of the spheres of philosophy and theology which had been so carefully explored in the middle ages. John Wenck, a professor at Heidelberg, raised a dissentient voice in his *De Ignota Litteratura*, but Nicholas showed no misgivings when making his reply in the *Apologia Doctae Ignorantiae*. It is evident that, by this time, the older scholastic philosophy had either to be brought back to life again and make a fresh beginning or to consent to fade away.

CHAPTER IX

THE RENAISSANCE AND LATER SCHOLASTICISM

§ 1

THE Renaissance was a great period in many ways, but it was not great in philosophy. Erasmus was typical of many of the humanists of the time in decrying scholasticism without either understanding it or offering any substitute for it. He succeeds at any rate in being amusing about it. While the philosophers pretend to explain nature, "Nature is meanwhile having a good laugh at them and their guesses. For, that nothing they say is really established, seems to be pretty well proved by the fact that they dispute interminably about everything. While they know nothing at all, they yet profess to know everything; ——they claim to perceive ideas, universals, separate forms, first matter, quiddities and thisnesses, things so tenuous that I do not believe even a lynx could make them out".[1]

Other humanists set out to revive the ancient systems, but rather in a literary way than with any profound metaphysical insight. There is a certain grace in the Platonism of Medici Florence, with Marsilio Ficino and Picodella Mirandola, but its objective results were a curious mixture of Platonism, Neoplatonism and occultism. Those who set out to discover an Aristotle unmodified by scholastic developments were philosophically more serious. Some, like Augustinus Niphus, merely saw Aristotle through the eyes of Averroes;

[1] Erasmus: *Praise of Folly*, ch. 52.

others, and especially Pomponatius, came much nearer to the genuine Aristotle and proceeded to throw doubt on the immortality of the individual soul.

There were yet other humanists who were not altogether unaware of the importance of the mediaeval achievement and were prepared to welcome its presentation in a more acceptable literary form. In the dialogue of Sadoleto *De Laudibus Philosophiae* we observe that his ambition was not to overthrow the traditional philosophy but to purify it from barbarism of expression and to make it intelligible in humanistic circles. Humanists of this kind joined hands with the scholastic revival which in fact took place in the early sixteenth century.

Then came the Reformation to complicate things still further. The Protestant movement may in its origins be not unfairly described as both anti-scholastic and anti-humanistic. Since Lutheranism had a primarily emotional inspiration, it was initially opposed to intellectualism of either variety. Anthony à Wood records a letter of Richard Layton to Thomas Cromwell in September 1535, describing what happened to the works of Scotus in the inauguration of the new order at Oxford. "We have set Dunce in Bocardo and have utterly banished him Oxford for ever with all his blind glosses; and he is now made a common servant to every man, fast nailed up upon posts in all common houses of easement—*id quod oculis meis vidi*. And the second time we came to New College after we had declared your injunctions, we found all the great Quadrant Court full of the leaves of Dunce, the wind blowing them into every corner." [1] As Protestantism spread and established itself, however, it naturally came to terms with both humanism and scholasticism. A Protestant cultivation of scholasticism began in Germany with Melanchthon, and scholastic philosophy continued to be taught at Cambridge until the middle of the seventeenth century and at Oxford even later.

§ 2

The storms of this period swept terminism away, although it did not obliterate all its effects. Thomism, however, and to some extent Scotism, entered upon a revival. Two celebrated Dominican commentators belong to the early years of the sixteenth century. Thomas de Vio, Cardinal Cajetan (1469-1534), composed, among other works, an elaborate commentary on the *Summa Theologica;* Sylvester Ferrariensis (*c.* 1474-1528) was the author of commentaries on the *Summa contra Gentiles* and on the *Physics* and *De Anima* of Aristotle. No interpreters of St. Thomas are held even to-day in greater honour.

The Spanish Dominicans made a resolute attempt to satisfy the stylistic exigences of the humanists. Francisco de Vittoria (1480-1546), whose most original contribution is some pioneering work on international relations, set the example in this direction, and was followed by Domingo de Soto and Melchior Cano. Another commentary on the *Summa Theologica* was the joint work of Medina and Bañez. The last distinguished representative of this Spanish Thomistic revival was John of

[1] *Cit. ap.* Longpré: *La Philosophie du B. Duns Scot,* p. 192 n.

St. Thomas (1589-1644), the author of a *Cursus Philosophicus ad exactam, veram et genuinam Aristotelis et doctoris angelici mentem.* This was the period when the distinction between philosophical truths, based on pure reason, and theological truths, based on divine revelation, a distinction clearly made by the great mediaeval thinkers, was recognized to the extent of systematically separating the course of philosophy from the course of theology.

Meanwhile the newly founded Society of Jesus began to be active in the intellectual field. Fonseca was the leading spirit in producing the philosophical course of Coimbra, consisting of elaborate commentaries on the works of Aristotle. Vasquez displayed an independent mind on a number of questions, especially in ethics. But the best-known of all the Jesuit philosophers of this epoch was Francisco Suarez (1548-1617), the author of *Disputationes Metaphysicae* and a treatise *De Legibus.* In the controversies of his time he was prominent, along with Bellarmine, in refuting James I's theory of the divine right of kings and upholding the mediaeval doctrine of the popular origin of sovereignty. Suarez was an eclectic rather than an original thinker, and Bossuet's remark that the whole of scholasticism finds an echo in him illustrates well enough both his merits and his limitations. Since the dominant note of his thinking is the attempt to arrive at a balance between the various opposed opinions, there is little which can be described as specifically Suarezian. But his arguments are always reasonable and his decisions judicious, so that Suarez remains a thinker worth consulting.

In general, this scholastic revival of the Renaissance

period was only a partial success. It produced no philosopher of the first class. The voluminous works written by its representatives consist for the most part of repetition of what greater minds had said better before them. The heart sinks as one handles these portentous folios. If only, one says to oneself, these people had set out to rethink their tradition from the beginning, and had been content to put down what they themselves had seen clearly and what had really interested and excited them! Even if they had not been great philosophers, they would then at least have been readable and worth reading. As it is, life being short, one replaces them on the shelf and takes up something less encyclopaedic and more original. That is, of course, what the men of the seventeenth century did. They took up the *Discours de la Méthode*, brief, lively and written in excellent French. But it is a pity that there was not someone of equal vigour on the side of the angels.

§ 3

There was, however, one point upon which a really lively controversy broke out among scholastic thinkers at this period. This was the nature of free will and its relation to the divine omnipotence. In so far as it was a theological controversy about grace, it falls outside our subject, but, since the springs of thought were in fact as much philosophical as theological, we are bound to treat of it from a philosophical point of view. In any case it would be unfair to leave it out, because it is a genuine breath of life which relieves the conventionality of the epoch.

We have already noted that the mediaeval authors did not carry the analysis of free will as far as they might have carried it. They were convinced of the reality of free will and moral responsibility, and they were convinced also of the universal causality and omnipotence of God. On how precisely these facts were to be fitted together St. Thomas does not seem to have made up his mind, nor does anyone else.

The difficulty was not in the reconciliation of free will with the eternal knowledge of God. That God in his eternal present sees our past, present and future, including future free acts, is a difficulty only for those who are unable to conceive eternity as it is, and think of it simply as unlimited time. This is, for the metaphysician at any rate, a rather obvious error, and one advantage of the continuous scholastic tradition in metaphysics was that it saved people from obvious errors of this kind. The real difficulty was in the relationship of free will to the divine causality. Was not God the cause of all being and of every element in it? Must he not then be the cause of our acts of will? If so, does he not causally determine all that we choose and do?

All the participants in this controversy maintained both the reality of free will and the reality of divine omnipotence. Hence there was no justification for scattering accusations of unorthodoxy, and the disputants were rightly restrained from doing so. The question was about the validity of the analyses by which they sought to fit these facts together.

In a larger context the controversy may be related to the emphasis laid by the Renaissance on individual man.

At this time men began to be more conscious of the rights of human personality. It was natural that more attention should be paid to the freedom of the will and consequent individual responsibility. Bañez and his followers held that St. Thomas had given a complete answer to the problem. Since God was the cause of all reality, he was the cause of our free acts too. Without a physical premotion from God our wills could not pass into act. As St. Thomas has said, it was the result of the very omnipotence of God that he could determine us to act freely and so to bring about what he willed in the manner appropriate to our nature. A paradox if you liked, a mystery certainly, but one which human reason could not overcome. You just had to leave it at that.

Molina and his followers held that Bañez was putting a full stop where St. Thomas had left a comma. What Aquinas had said was true, but it left room for further inquiry. Molina, representing in this respect the spirit of the Renaissance, thought that the time for further inquiry had come. If free will were a reality, it entailed that our free acts came in some ultimate sense from ourselves. It was not enough that end and circumstances did not determine volition; the will must really determine itself. What, then, became of divine providence? Did God have to wait upon the decisions of his creatures? In order to avoid this difficulty, Molina excogitated the theory of *scientia media*. It was recognized that God had an essential knowledge of all possibilities and a knowledge of all facts which he had decreed to come to pass. Between these two types of knowledge Molina placed *scientia media,* a knowledge of all that a free agent would do if he were created. Hence, in creating a free agent, God knew what his volitions would be, and the domination of divine providence was preserved.

Bañez and his followers retorted by asking how there could be this knowledge of hypothetical free acts. If a free act were thus known apart from its actual occurrence, it could only be because it was determined by the circumstances. Therefore Molina, in seeking to uphold free will, had plunged straight into psychological determinism. Molina replied by asserting that Bañez, with his theory of physical premotion, made God the author of sin and would logically be led to deny free will altogether. He saved himself only by taking refuge in a mystery, but this was much less a mystery than a contradiction.

The controversy raged for many years at the end of the sixteenth and the beginning of the seventeenth century, but neither side could convince the other. Indeed, both views are still held now with equal firmness as then, if not with equal passion. An historian may be permitted to suggest that the disputants were more successful in criticizing each other than in establishing their positive opinions. It is certainly very difficult to see how there could be *scientia media* without psychological determinism. At the same time it seems that our consciousness of moral responsibility could hardly be what it is unless some acts at least were free in a more intensive sense than any which Bañez would admit. The last word has not been said on this subject.

§ 4

After this bright interlude it falls to our lot to account for the final collapse of mediaeval scholasticism. We have seen that the scholastics of the seventeenth century were not such as to communicate a thrill to the inquiring mind. Nevertheless they were, in their somewhat humdrum way, transmitting a tradition of thought which might have been of very considerable use to the philosophers who came after them. Why is it that these philosophers, on the whole, paid no attention to them?

The answer to this question lies in a change in the direction of human interest. There was, first of all, a change in the direction of philosophical inquiry. However much the sources of Descartes' thought are investigated and his debts to mediaeval thinkers brought to light, it is still true that he was trying to do something different from what his predecessors had intended. The full epistemological approach to philosophy comes into existence with Descartes. Henceforth the philosopher had to presuppose nothing, to uncover the primitive data of thought, and to build his system explicitly upon what he conceived to be absolutely irrefragable foundations. Until the foundations had been tested, even the most imposing constructions began to appear as potential candidates for demolition.

Furthermore, the seventeenth century saw the rise of modern physical science. Men began to see the possibility of increasing their knowledge of the material world by more extended observation, and still more by the invention of more exact methods of observation. With the application of mathematics, emphasis shifted from the qualitative to the quantitative aspects of nature. While in our own country Bacon contributed something to the new conceptions, it was even more the work of Galileo in Italy to inaugurate the change. The physical sciences in those days were still known as natural philosophy, and this was the part of philosophy to which a great number of the most active thinkers devoted their attention.

Interest, therefore, was moving away from the kind of question which had absorbed the mediaeval philosophers and the kind of method which they had used. To this challenge the seventeenth-century scholastics made no reply. Set in their ways, they went on placidly as if the novelties were of no importance. The professor at Padua who refused to look through Galileo's telescope was, no doubt, an extreme example, but he was an extreme example of a common type. Just occasionally, as in John of St. Thomas, one finds an increased solicitude about the problems of knowledge, but no scholastic offered an equally thorough criticism of experience which could hold the field against the system of Descartes.

The inevitable consequence followed. Since the scholastics let the world go by, the world revenged itself by forgetting about them. Scholastic philosophy lingered on as a set of notions to serve as an introduction to theology, but it had no living contact with any other department of thought. The survival of mediaeval terminology provided a rather ineffectual reminder to Catholics that theology had once been an integral part of a whole edifice of knowledge, human and divine, but it was now left high and dry. The only reason why scholasticism did not altogether disappear was that no later system seemed readily to harmonize with theology at all.

Meanwhile an occasional philosopher, like Sir William Hamilton, had taken the trouble to read the schoolmen and had pointed out that they were not as bad as they were painted by those who did not take this trouble. By the middle of the nineteenth century it became fairly apparent that the new methods of philosophizing were not likely by themselves to issue in any satisfactory positive system. At last it occurred to Catholics to take the philosophy of the Christian middle ages seriously again. There followed the scholastic revival, which has gradually gathered force and momentum and which, if it is not yet much noticed in England, is nevertheless an important ingredient in the philosophical life of the Continent. It is not our function to deal with it here, but the increasing attention paid by European philosophers to mediaeval thought should at least be mentioned.

§ 5

The reader who has been through this brief survey of mediaeval philosophy will also be asking himself whether what he has read is merely ancient history or has it some relevance to his own philosophical thinking. If we wish to maintain the latter alternative, we ought to indicate what this relevance is and under what conditions it can be appreciated.

In the first place, if you want to utilize mediaeval thought, you have to arrive at a solution of the epistemological problems which have preoccupied philosophers since Descartes. If you are an adherent of the new nominalism, and think that philosophy is merely a glorified theory of language, you may be mildly entertained by seeing an approximation to this position in William of Ockham, but you will have no ground from which you can make a start in the fruitful understanding of the more typical mediaeval thinkers. If your are a realist but think that the only realities with which we are acquainted are sense-data, you will likewise be inclined to dismiss the scholastic systems as baseless conceptual constructions. You must first convince yourself that thought is not simply refined sensation, and that we are really acquainted with persons and things; then the mediaeval philosophies will have a meaning for you. Perhaps we may venture to assert that it is not quite so difficult to acquire this conviction as it is sometimes supposed to be.

When the problems of knowledge are once settled in principle, it becomes evident that the proper range of philosophical speculation includes a great many subjects beyond epistemology. You will want a metaphysic or ontology in the sense of an analysis of the most general and fundamental notions such as being, substance and cause. And you will want to apply this analysis to the discussion of those perennial subjects of human interest which are the nature of man and the existence and nature of absolute being. Here you will find the greatest help in the logical rigour and sobriety with which the mediaeval thinkers approach these problems, about which the modern man is so often content to feel deeply and be profoundly convinced instead of thinking hard.

If you are a Christian, or at least have some sympathy with Christianity, you will find a special interest in the philosophical systems which grew up in intimate communication with the Christian faith. You may experience a sense of emancipation in discovering that doctrines which are nowadays too frequently matters either of emotional acceptance or of emotional rejection were discussed in the middle ages with the dispassionate exactness of a laundry list. You will find that theology can be treated as a science. But it should be stressed once again that the mediaeval scholastics made a clear distinction between the field of human reason and the field of divine revelation. They were philosophers in the full sense as well as theologians. A respect for their theology may create an initial sympathy with their philosophy, but the grounds on which their philosophical opinions have to be discussed are entirely independent of their theology.

It is not a question of restoring a solid block of thinking without change or addition. In any case, there is not a mediaeval philosophy but there are mediaeval philosophies; although there is a larger measure of agreement among the most important mediaeval thinkers than is common in modern philosophy, they differed from one another on a great many points and disputed lustily. Nor, obviously, do they invalidate what has been thought and discovered since their time. We have already mentioned the necessity of a criticism of experience of which they never dreamed; there is also the whole mass of modern physical and psychological investigation to be brought into an organic relationship with the metaphysical framework which they provided.

And that is precisely where collaboration might be most fruitful. While, in psychology for example, the mediaeval metaphysical framework may seem to the contemporary mind imposing but rather empty, modern psychology presents us with a chaotic mass of observations and speculations which plainly need some such framework for their real meaning to appear and their value to be appreciated.

Hence it is worth commending the study of mediaeval philosophy as relevant to contemporary thinking. The mediaeval mind is in so many ways different from the modern that an historical introduction is indispensable, but this should be the prelude to a positive utilization of its products. There is much more than the satisfaction of historical curiosity in making the acquaintance of Bonaventure and Duns Scotus and, above all, Thomas Aquinas.

A SELECT LIST OF BOOKS

THE purpose of this section is not to provide the scholar with an elaborate bibliography but, by mentioning a few important works, to help the student to prosecute his researches in mediæval philosophy a little farther. The needs of the English reader have been borne in mind by giving preference, as far as possible, to English works or translations, but foreign books are listed when they are of the first importance or when there is nothing in English covering the same ground. The latter reason holds good with regrettable frequency.

The standard survey is by M. de Wulf: *Histoire de la Philosophie Médiévale* (5th ed., 2 vols., 1924–5; 6th ed., of which two volumes, reaching the end of the thirteenth century, appeared in 1934 and 1936). Of this there is an English translation by E.C. Messenger (*History of Mediæval Philosophy*). Fuller bibliographies can be found in the relevant volume of F. Ueberweg: *Grundriss der Geschichte der Philosophie, II, Die Patristische und Scholastische Philosophie* (last ed. by B. Geyer, 1928). For a stimulating summary E. Gilson: *La Philosophie au Moyen Age* (Collection Payot) can be recommended.

Gilson, whose combination of exact scholarship and philosophical insight makes him the leading contemporary mediævalist, has produced the best survey of what mediæval philosophy is about in his Gifford lectures on *L'Esprit de la Philosophie Médiévale*. This work has been translated into English by A. H. C. Downes (*The Spirit of Mediæval Philosophy*) Of Gilson, see also chapter II, on "God and Christian Philosophy", of his book on *God and Philosophy*.

Another useful general work is by M. de Wulf: *Civilization and Philosophy in the Middle Ages*. A number of studies are brought together in R. L. Poole: *Illustrations of the History of Mediæval Thought and Learning*. The English

reader has also H. O. Taylor: *The Mediæval Mind*. A less
sympathetic standpoint can be represented by F. Picavet:
*Esquisse d'une Histoire Générale et Comparée des Philoso-
phies Médiévales* and by E. Bréhier: *La Philosophie du
Moyen Age*. On particular aspects we have the great work of
M. Grabmann: *Geschichte der scholastischen Methode* (2
vols., unfinished) and a short but useful *Geschichte der
Gottesbeweise im Mittelalter*, by G. Grunwald.

The student should be acquainted with the principal
series in which studies of mediæval thought appear. These
are the *Beiträge zur Geschichte der Philosophie des Mittelalters* (Münster, ed. M. Grabmann), *Etudes de Philosophie
Médiévale* (Paris, ed. E. Gilson) and *Bibliothèque Thomiste*
(Paris). In recent years a number of short texts of mediæval
thinkers have been issued, especially in the series *Opuscula
et textus historiam Ecclesiae eiusque vitam atque doctrinam
illustrantia, series scholastica* (Münster, ed. M. Grabmann
and F. Pelster) and *Textus et documenta in usum exercita-
tionum et praelectionum academicarum, series philosophica*
(Rome, Gregorian University).

The most accessible edition of Boethius will probably be
the volume of the Loeb Classical Library containing the
Tracts and *De Consolatione Philosophiæ*, ed. and trans.
H. F. Stewart and E. K. Rand. There is an excellent critical
edition of the *De Consolatione*, with editorial matter in
Latin, by A. Fortescue and G. Smith. The complete works of
Boethius can, of course, be found in Migne: *Patrologia
Latina* (vol. 63), and a presumably final critical edition of
the *De Consolatione*, by G. Weinberger, has appeared in the
Corpus Scriptorum Ecclesiasticorum Latinorum (Vienna).
On Boethius the English reader had until recently nothing
but H. F. Stewart's early and not entirely adequate essay
(*Boethius*), but of late years there have appeared *Boethius*,
by H. M. Barrett, and *The Tradition of Boethius*, by H. R.
Patch. The first part of Rocco Murari: *Dante e Boezio* deals
exclusively with Boethius, and is admirable.

The works of Erigena are in Migne: *Pat. Lat.*, vol. 122,
and an introduction to his thought is provided by Henry
Bett: *Johannes Scotus Erigena*. Anselm can be found in
Migne, vols. 158–9, but there are now handy editions of the

Monologion and *Proslogion*, ed. F. S. Schmitt, in the series *Florilegium Patristicum* (Bonn), and, under the title of *Fides Quærens Intellectum*, a volume containing the *Proslogion, Liber Gaunilonis pro Insipiente* and *Liber Apologeticus contra Gaunilonem*, ed. with French trans. by A. Koyré in the series *Bibliothèque des Textes Philosophiques* (Paris). See also Domet de Vorges: *St. Anselme*, and A. Koyré: *L'Idée de Dieu dans la Philosophie de St. Anselme*.

A good general account of the twelfth-century movement is due to C. H. Haskins: *The Renaissance of the Twelfth Century*. Abelard deserves a renewal of attention. For most of his works we have still to refer to the edition of Victor Cousin, which is more than a century old, although his logical writings have recently received a critical edition from B. Geyer in the *Beiträge zur Geschichte der Philosophie des Mittelalters*. Cf. J. G. Sikes: *Peter Abailard*. C. C. J. Webb has written on *John of Salisbury* with the acumen to be expected of the editor of the *Policraticus* and *Metalogicon*. On the mediæval organization of teaching, the English reader has *The Universities of Europe in the Middle Ages*, by Dr. Hastings Rashdall.

On the Arabs, cf. De Lacy O'Leary: *Arabic Thought and its Place in History*. The task of dealing adequately with mediæval translations of the ancient philosophers is only in its beginning. The first part of *Aristoteles Latinus*, by G. Lacombe, classifying the manuscripts of translations of Aristotle, appeared at Rome in 1939. The *Corpus Platonicum Medii Aevi*, ed. R. Klibansky, is sponsored by the Warburg Institute of London; an introduction to the work to be accomplished is given by Klibansky in *The Continuity of the Platonic Tradition during the Middle Ages*.

D. A. Callus has written recently on the *Introduction of Aristotelian Learning to Oxford* (Proceedings of the British Academy, vol. xxix). In her *Franciscan Philosophy at Oxford in the Thirteenth Century* D. E. Sharp deals with Robert Grosseteste, Thomas of York, Roger Bacon, Richard of Middleton, John Peckham and Duns Scotus. The works of Roger Bacon have been appearing at intervals under the care of R. Steele and others. On thirteenth-century Averroism, the standard work of P. Mandonnet: *Siger de Brabant et l'Averroisme Latin,* can now be supplemented by F. Van Steenberghen: *Les Oeuvres et la Doctrine de Siger de Brabant.*

The Franciscans of Quaracchi have produced a critical edition of the works of St. Bonaventure (1882-1902). A handier edition of the most important writings has been set on foot, beginning with the commentary on the first two books of the *Sentences.* From Quaracchi, too, comes a useful small volume containing the *Breviloquium, Itinerarium Mentis in Deum* and *De Reductione Artium ad Theologiam.* An introductory selection of texts has been compiled by B. Rosenmöller: *Philosophia S. Bonaventuræ textibus ex eius operibus selectis illustrata (Opuscula et Textus, series scholastica, fasc. xv.)* By far the best book on this doctor is E. Gilson: *La Philosophie de St. Bonaventure.* This has been translated into English by I. Trethowan and F. J. Sheed *(The Philosophy of St. Bonaventure).*

The writings of St. Thomas Aquinas are relatively easy to obtain. The best text so far available is to be found in the Leonine edition (Rome, still incomplete), and the *Summa contra Gentiles* has been reissued in this text in a handier form. B. Roland-Gosselin's edition of the *De Ente et Essentia* contains much useful editorial matter. The English Dominicans have produced a translation of the *Summa Theologica.* Thomas Aquinas: *Selected Writings* (Everyman's Library) is a rather disconnected collection of extracts. E. Gilson: *St. Thomas d'Aquin,* in the series *Les Moralistes Chrétiens,* contains extracts in French from St. Thomas's ethical writings with editorial connecting links, and is extremely well done.

M. C. D'Arcy: *Thomas Aquinas,* can be thoroughly recommended. E. Gilson: *Le Thomisme,* has been translated as *The Philosophy of St. Thomas Aquinas,* and M. Grabmann: *Thomas von Aquin* as *Thomas Aquinas, his Personality and Thought.* Another important book which has been translated is P. Rousselot: *The Intellectualism of St. Thomas (L'Int. de St. Th.)*; Rousselot was too original a thinker to be a pure historian, but he is all the more interesting on that account. Cf. also R. L. Patterson: *The Conception of God in the Philosophy of Aquinas.*

In contrast with Aquinas, it is somewhat difficult to achieve an adequate conception of Duns Scotus. The classical edition of his works by Luke Wadding (1639, reprinted 1891) contains many writings which are spurious and a corrupt text of the genuine writings. A critical edition, which will be a boon, is in preparation by the Franciscans, but the difficulties in the way are expounded by C. Balic in *Les Commentaires de Jean Duns Scot sur les quatre livres des Sentences*. Meanwhile the best information about Scotus is to be obtained from E. Longpré: *La Philosophie du B. Duns Scot*, which is in form a polemic against B. Landry's perverse work on the same subject, and from Déodat de Basly: *Scotus Docens*, a brief synthesis of his teaching with valuable extracts. In English, C. R. S. Harris, *Duns Scotus*, is unfortunately based largely on works now known to be spurious. Cf. review of it by E. Gilson in *Mind*, Jan. 1928.

J. Koch: *Durandus de S. Porciano*, in German, is our principal source of information on this thinker. E. A. Moody: *The Logic of William of Ockham*, is a work of exact scholarship. H. Rashdall wrote on "Nicholas de Ulticuria, a mediæval Hume" in the *Proceedings of the Aristotelian Society*, 1907. Otto Gierke: *Political Theories of the Middle Age*, trans. by F. W. Maitland, is, especially in its notes, a pretty complete guide to the literature of the subject.

A considerable part has appeared of an edition of both the Latin and the German works of Eckhart, sponsored by the Deutsche Forschungsgemeinschaft. An edition of the Latin works was also begun under the auspices of the Dominicans of Santa Sabina (Rome). B. J. Muller Thym has written *On the University of Being in Meister Eckhart of Hochheim*. A new edition of Nicholas of Cusa was also in progress under the care of the Heidelberg Akademie der Wissenschaften. Meanwhile there is a handy edition of the *De Docta Ignorantia* by P. Rotta. E. Vansteenberghe has written in French on *Nicolas de Cues*, while Henry Bett: *Nicholas of Cusa*, provides an English account of this author.

Of the later scholastics of whom modern editions have appeared we may mention Suarez, Vittoria (*De Indis et de*

Jure Belli), Molina (*Concordia Liberi Arbitrii cum Gratia*) and John of St. Thomas (*Cursus Philosophicus*). Finally we should not omit to mention the two small volumes of extracts in English from *Mediæval Philosophy*, ed. by R. McKeon in the Modern Student's Library. Books about the philosophers of the middle ages are needed, but acquaintance should be made as soon as possible with their actual writings.

INDEX